MAMA MADE THE DIFFERENCE

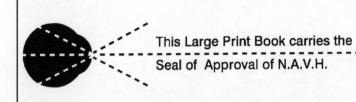

This Large Print Book carries the
Seal of Approval of N.A.V.H.

MAMA MADE THE DIFFERENCE
LIFE LESSONS MY MOTHER TAUGHT ME

T. D. JAKES

THORNDIKE PRESS

An imprint of Thomson Gale, a part of The Thomson Corporation

THOMSON

GALE

Detroit • New York • San Francisco • New Haven, Conn. • Waterville, Maine • London • Munich

Thorndike Press® Large Print African-American.

The text of this Large Print edition is unabridged.

Other aspects of the book may vary from the original edition.

Set in 16 pt. Plantin.

LIBRARY OF CONGRESS CATALOGING-IN-PUBLICATION DATA

Jakes, T. D.
    Mama made the difference : life lessons my mother taught me / by T.D. Jakes. — Large print ed.
        p. cm.
    Includes bibliographical references.
    ISBN 0-7862-8868-X (lg. print : hardcover : alk. paper) 1. Motherhood — Religious aspects — Christianity. 2. African Americans — Religion. 3. Large type books. I. Title.
BV4529.18.J35 2006b
248.8'431—dc22   2006014980

Published in 2006 by arrangement with G. P. Putnam's Sons, a division of Penguin Group (USA) Inc.

Printed in the United States of America on permanent paper
10 9 8 7 6 5 4 3 2 1

For my wife, Serita,
the mother of my children
For my mama, Mrs. Odith P. Jakes,
the mother of who I have become
For Coretta Scott King,
the mother of the civil rights movement

The church sanctuary was adorned with enough roses and lilies to fill two florists' shops. The aisles overflowed with people dark-clad in the colors of mourning — men and women, black and white, young and old, rich and poor, the famous and the infamous, as well as those unknown to the public eye. The nation's power brokers bowed their heads in respect, seated alongside those able to lift their heads with pride every day, knowing they would be politically powerless without the efforts of the woman we were there to celebrate.

As I surveyed the throng of mourners, I counted among our number four living presidents: President George W. Bush, along with First Lady Laura Bush; Bill Clinton; George H. W. Bush; and Jimmy Carter. A host of great singers, including one featured in this book, CeCe Winans, along with her brother BeBe Winans, the incomparable

Stevie Wonder, and a choir of accomplished musicians, provided a remarkable offering of commemorative spirituals and hymns that captured the gratitude and grief, the passion and purpose of the woman we had come to honor: Mrs. Coretta Scott King.

I recalled how on my last visit with her we didn't dine together as we often had; her health was declining and the stroke had hampered her speech. Still, she managed to communicate enough with me to inspire me as we prayed together.

Just as this book was going to press, Mrs. King passed from this life with the same grace and dignity with which she lived it. Coming less than a year after the loss of another civil rights pioneer, Rosa Parks, the death of the Reverend King's cochampion of equality and justice reminded us that while the torch of equal rights has been passed, we have not fully illuminated all the dark corners of prejudice and racism. As we embrace the expansive legacy of this re-markable woman, this icon of an era in our nation's history, it seems such a providential gift to have her daughter Bernice, who delivered such a beautiful eulogy at this service, share firsthand a glimpse of her mother later in this book.

What I set out to do in writing this book

is simple: to pay homage to the incredible gifts of our mothers and to offer tribute to the wise lessons that they pass on to us. I learned many of the lessons that I share with you in this book from my own mother, a strong and resilient woman of grace whose absence continues to echo in the canyons of my heart each day. But I also observed the lessons contained here from other mothers such as Mrs. King.

And like so many women who may not be our biological mothers but who become our spiritual, emotional, and psychological mothers, Mrs. King demonstrated the lessons she held most dear by the way she lived her life. Carrying on her husband's legacy. Overcoming barriers of fear and distrust. Upholding the practical impact of equal rights for all people. Whether she was speaking at a council of world leaders, counseling a group of at-risk young women, inspiring generosity at an educational fund-raiser, or lobbying to remove the wrenching stigma of the past, she made a difference.

Yes, like so many remarkable mothers, Coretta Scott King made a difference. Certainly she affected the lives of her children: Yolanda, Martin III, Bernice, and Dexter. But she also generously left in the lives of many others a substantial deposit that will continue to flow forward for many generations. And so, as I offer this book to her, as well as to my own mother and the mother of my children, I pray that all who read these pages may be ignited by Mrs. King's example to make their own life-changing, soul-liberating difference in the lives of those around them. I dedicate this book then not just to my mother, my wife, and Mrs. King, but to all the women who will read it and realize that each person they touch is potentially the next one to change the world. Thank you for being the hand that rocks the cradle. Through those you touch, you will rule the world.

CONTENTS

11

PART THREE
GRADUATION DAY: LESSONS ON
LONGEVITY FROM OUR GREATEST

ACKNOWLEDGMENTS

Just as the collective wisdom of so many mothers went into the lessons of this book, similarly the combined efforts of so many others contributed to its writing. I am deeply grateful for the time, energy, love, and prayers of those who supported my personal and professional infrastructure during the completion of these pages. As the joyful craziness of my schedule continues to take its toll, I don't know what I'd do without you! Thank you for the investment in my vision for this project in ways that will continue to make a difference.

I owe a debt of loving gratitude to my wife, Serita, whose grace and patience as the mother of my children is second only to her beauty and passion as my wife. To my children, thank you for providing the laboratory in which so many of these lessons have been tested. I pray that they serve you well for years to come and will be worthy of your passing along to your children.

My thanks to Denise Silvestro, a devoted and tireless champion of making my message the best it can be. Her dexterous skill and thoughtful heart helped put my ideas, observations, and experiences into words. If this book sings like I hope it does, then it stays in tune because of her contribution.

Joel Fotinos continues to provide me with encouragement, enthusiasm, and insight. His passion for my message and his trust in my methods are precious gifts not taken for granted.

Thank you to everyone at Putnam. You took my vision to new heights and helped it soar. My sincere thanks to Ivan Held, Doug Jones, Susan Petersen Kennedy, Marilyn Ducksworth, Dick Heffernan, Chris Mosley, Katie Day, and everyone at Strang Communications and the Noble Group.

Special thanks to Beth Clark for her literary abilities and catalytic contributions. Without her insight and suggestions, this book would not be as strong. And to Dudley Delffs, whose expertise enhanced my ideas and added so much to this project.

Finally, to all the mothers out there who have infused my life with your wisdom and wonder, I thank you.

16

INTRODUCTION

TIMELESS TEACHERS IN THE CLASSROOM OF LIFE

I'll never forget the feeling of entering that room for the first time. After walking down the hill from my house with my mother, I strolled nervously down the long, never-ending hallway amidst the chattering bustle of others my size and many more who were much larger than my boyhood frame. Nervousness, excitement, a little fear, and a large dose of curiosity infused my system with a powerful elixir. Inside the room that would become a kind of second home to me for the next nine months, I scanned the brightly colored bulletin boards, the blackboard that dominated an entire wall, the green border above it with its neatly scrolled alphabet letters that I would soon be expected to master, the many rows of desks and chairs that were just my size. The place smelled of chalk dust and ammonia, laced with the scent of daisies from the bouquet on the teacher's desk and perhaps just a hint of her sweet perfume. As I peered in, other curious faces looked back at me, each of them just as eager and terrified as I was on this first day of school. Mrs. Dills looked up at me and smiled, and I felt that school might not be so bad after all. At that moment I let go of my mother's hand, she who had guided me through the labyrinthine halls of this new, strange, and exhilarating locale, and stepped forward with the same sense of monumental achievement as the first man on the moon!

Who can forget their introduction into the education system? We all had to take that first big step toward maturity and intellectual stimulation, a step that would shape and craft us into a smarter version of ourselves. Perhaps it was easier for me because my mother was a teacher, both by profession but also by her very nature. She couldn't pass up any opportunity — and they were abundant each day — to share with others her contagious curiosity about everything around her. She handed out lessons to those of us around her the way a millionaire hands out tips!

Because of the life lessons that Mama had already started teaching me, I quickly felt at home in my new classroom. I discovered that I was used to paying attention to each day's lessons because my mother had already instilled in me an appreciation of information, knowledge, and most precious of all, wisdom. In fact, my mother had already shared her view that life itself is the classroom that God gives us to learn who we are, who He is, and how we are to become who He created us to be. I learned some of life's most important lessons long before I entered first grade. This proclivity toward lifelong learning continues to be one of the most significant legacies my mother left me.

Thinking about my mother and the many other mothers I know, along with numerous observations and experiences gleaned from other people about their mothers, I think it's time to pay tribute to these most influential of educators — our mamas. I believe the time is right to examine the legacy that our mothers continue to bequeath to us, and to heed their lessons as we move forward into our own God-given destinies. It's not just that our mothers' wisdom is timeless, but that it's especially timely today, in our twenty-first century.

You see, I've witnessed a growing apathy toward motherhood. With all of our many advances in technology and corporate culture, women are now expected to excel in the boardroom as well as the kitchen. The woman who doesn't wish to work outside her home is often looked down upon as being old-fashioned or incapable of the immense juggling act that her sisters enact around her.

But we need mothers, along with their luminous lessons that shine across the shadows of time, more than ever. Women should not have to apologize for being mothers. As a society, we're in trouble when we don't value our children enough to place them above our careers, our leisure activities, or our goals of self-improvement. No, we must step back and realize that mothers have often shaped our world from the cradle, by rocking, nurturing, and instructing children who grow up to make life-changing and history-making accomplishments. For every radical revolutionary or fast-forward fashionista, every preacher and president, every molecular scientist and Internet technician, there's a mother behind them who fostered her child's sensibilities to their full potential.

Have you ever considered the way your mother has shaped the person you are today? Learning from our mothers — whether they are biological, emotional, or spiritual mothers to us — is something that all of us share. You see, everybody has a mother, whether it's the hardened criminal on death row, or the successful executive on Wall Street. Heads of state and heads of major corporations all entered this world through the painful labor of a woman. And if that woman didn't raise and nurture them, then there was likely another woman — an aunt, a big sister, a church mother — who loved them as her own. Indeed, if there is one thing every member of the human race has in common with all others, it is that each one of us is someone's child. We all began our life's journey in a woman's womb. All of us who live and have ever lived came into being through a woman, to whom God said, "I need you to assist me in the miracle of life." He trusts mothers so much that He allows them to share in His creative work. Mothers are the banks into which God has chosen to deposit life. It's been that way since the very first birth on earth and it is still that way all over the planet.

The vital role that mothers play has not diminished over time, but our perception of mothers has shifted dramatically. Consider for a moment the way we have watched the image of motherhood evolve on the screens of our television sets. We have seen the glories and the challenges of motherhood portrayed in Caroline Ingalls, Olivia Walton, Aunt Bee, June Cleaver, and Carol Brady, to name a few. But the days of *Leave It to Beaver* and *The Brady Bunch* are no more. Rarely will you find a woman who cleans house *and* bakes pies and cookies *every* single day. You are less likely to stumble upon a lady who starches both her aprons and the bedsheets of her entire household. In fact, if you were to knock on the doors of one hundred households, you would find only thirty women who could be called "stay-at-home moms."

No, mothers today work inside the home, outside the home, and everywhere in between as they shuttle between their kids' school, the church, and their office, not to mention the grocery store and dry cleaner. According to an *ABC News* original report on May 8, 2005, 70 percent of mothers who have children under the age of eighteen balance outside employment with their duties at home. The same report cites that 61.8 percent of mothers with children under the age of six have jobs outside the home. The television mothers many of us grew up with did not work. Oh, there was at least one *Andy Griffith* episode in which Aunt Bee secured a job, but by the time the ending credits rolled, she was happily back in her kitchen to stay!

In 1984, our perception of mothers, at least the characters we saw on our television screens, began to change with the introduction of a trailblazing working mother in the character of Clair Huxtable on *The Cosby Show*. Clair was the mother of five children, whose ages ranged from elementary school to post-college. She was a devoted mother, able to provide insight and wisdom to her children when needed and to keep a perfect house, all while maintaining her position as a busy attorney. Sure, we can admire Clair Huxtable for being able to perform a difficult job while raising a healthy, thriving family, but she is not a realistic example of a working mother. Most working mothers struggle with feelings of guilt because they are unable to be with their children as much as stay-at-home moms can. In addition, they sometimes face criticism, wage discrimination, and severe time constraints. And many working mothers have what works out to be at least two full-time jobs — bringing home the bacon *and* having to fry it up in a pan.

However, working moms are not the only ones who struggle today. Young mothers, those who become pregnant as teenagers and even preteens, are also a great concern.

In the year 2000, eighty-three of every one thousand teenage girls in America got pregnant. In 2002, girls between the ages of ten and fourteen gave birth to 7,315 babies. The number of teenage pregnancies in America is declining, but it is still alarming.

Our children are having children. And if it is difficult to raise children, think how much harder it is when you are just a child yourself. Some young women who found themselves pregnant have had abortions; some have given their babies up for adoption; some have tried to hide; some have failed miserably as they struggled to raise a child for whom they were unprepared. On the other hand, some say they have been successful, usually because they have had extralarge doses of help, compassion, and wisdom from people who cared too much to let them fail.

On the other end of the spectrum from teenage mothers we see women becoming first-time mothers at thirty, thirty-five, forty, forty-two, forty-four — even some who have made news when they gave birth in their fifties and their sixties. As Americans, we are living longer than we once did and we have longer sexual lives resulting from better health in general — and from pharmaceutical innovations like Viagra! Such factors allow for an extension of the typical understanding of "childbearing years."

Where our teenage mothers lack so much of the vital life experience that time affords, older mothers have experience overload. In many cases, these women are financially secure and they do not share the economic concerns of their young counterparts, but their challenges are social. It's not easy to hear comments about your adorable grandchild every time you go to the supermarket if that "grandchild" is your own newborn son or daughter. Their challenges are also physical: come on, at forty, who doesn't suffer from a midlife energy crisis! Unlike their teenage counterparts, most older mothers don't have to worry about having enough money to support their children, they have to worry about having enough energy to keep up with them. They don't have to worry about how to finish college while caring for an infant, but they wonder if their own health will hold out so they can see their sons and daughters graduate someday.

And many moms today are raising their children alone. The U.S. Census Bureau reports that there were 10.1 million single mothers in the United States in 2003, an increase from 7.5 million in the 2000 census. Some of these women are single because they have chosen not to marry, some have lost their spouses to death or divorce, and some have been abandoned. One reason single mothers often find life so difficult is that they are the sole breadwinners for their families and must work full-time. One of their ongoing obstacles is time management. Simply finding time to do everything that must be done for everyone in the household can seem impossible.

Another reason some single mothers struggle is that, deep in their hearts, they long for companionship. Some will even proudly admit that they are "on the hunt." A woman has a dilemma when she says yes to the call of mothering while she is lonely for male attention. She needs to know that callings have sacrifices. A woman cannot mother well if she is always going on dates. Motherhood does not prohibit a relationship with a man, it simply means that instead of expending all of her energy searching for Mr. Right, she needs to trust God to bring someone to her who fits her situation. While she waits for Him, she needs to find appropriate, healthy ways to deal with her longings and her loneliness while fulfilling her responsibilities to her children.

As you can see, motherhood now glistens

with so many different facets in the dawn of our new century. Some aspects of mothering are easier than they were for women thirty years ago, and some are more challenging. Modern conveniences and technology have simultaneously increased both the productivity and the pressure in our lives. *Things* are easier to manage, but *time* seems more difficult. Decentralized families and day-care centers have changed the way women mother and the way children perceive their mothers.

But for all the changes motherhood has undergone in its long, storied history, some maternal dynamics remain the same. For instance, we still want our mothers when we're sick, mothers still know when "something is wrong," and there's still nothing quite as comforting as having our mother's arms wrapped around us when we're sad, lonely, or afraid. And, ultimately, mothers remain some of our most powerful teachers in the hands-on laboratory of everyday living.

What makes for these timeless qualities of a mother? Of all their many attributes, I believe that it all comes down to the heart — a mother's heart, to be exact. It really has nothing to do with biology or reproductive science; it has everything to do with the tenderness and toughness, the compassion and conscientiousness, of the heart. Not everyone can bear children physically (particularly men!), but everyone knows something of what it means to birth a dream, a goal, a hope. We learn innately what it means to nurture and tend, to care for and comfort, to build up and lean into by experiencing the ways our mothers loved us.

My own mother was a most remarkable person. She embodies the reasons that I esteem mothers so highly. In fact, when people ask me why much of my nearly thirty-year ministry has focused on seeing women healed and released into everything God has for them, I tell them that my loving and ministering to women is born of the way I loved and appreciated my mother. I am who I am today in large part because of my mother, and I have written this book on behalf of all the sons and daughters who know they are who they are because of their mother. I have penned these pages in honor — in celebration and in tribute — of every mother who has ever lived.

And it's not only that we need to be reminded of our mothers' timeless truths. I want all the mothers out there to know how much their sacrifices matter, how much what they teach us really does make a difference. Mothers need to be told how much we appreciate all that they have imparted to us in their various lessons, to know that we love and cherish their wisdom, and that we would never be where we are without their support and encouragement. I travel very often, and I seldom go into a city in which someone does not say to me, "My mother loves you, Bishop Jakes!" I suppose, more than any other comment, I hear about the mothers who appreciate my ministry. One of the reasons I have written this book is to say, "Mothers, I love you too!"

In this book, I am delighted to pass along some of my mother's advice and wisdom that has encouraged and ministered to me, to share of my own observations, experiences, and thoughts about motherhood, and to pass along to you some of the great lessons my mama and other mothers taught me about life, love, and longevity. Portraits of other mothers, some of whom you will know and some you will read about for the first time, are also included as "Substitute Teachers" within each of the three sections of this book. When my friends and colleagues discovered that I was writing about the lessons I learned from my mama, they were eager to tell me about their own special maternal relationships, and I'm delighted to include their stories here in celebration of the women who have played such vital roles in making them the people they are today.

I hope you will be encouraged and empowered as you read; I hope you will glean your own life lessons from what we share in this book. I hope you will be inspired to birth the greatness that has already been planted in your life and to share your fruits of the journey with those around you. And, somewhere along the way, I hope you will take a moment to remember and to honor your mother, realizing afresh that you are who you are today because Mama made the difference in your life.

■ ■ ■ ■

PART ONE
HOMEROOM:
LESSONS ON LIFE
FROM OUR GREATEST
TEACHERS

■ ■ ■ ■

Can you remember the first time you realized that your mother might actually know what she was talking about? That she wasn't just trying to control your life and dominate your decisions with her omniscient awareness of every cookie you sneaked or every chore you forgot to complete? Our mothers' admonitions and prohibitions tend to linger in our minds long after the sound of their voices reminding us of our curfew has faded.

I recall being a young man caught in the cusp between childhood and adulthood, a young teenager desperate to test my limitations and fit in with my friends. On this particular occasion, the only thing standing between me and my freedom was the dreaded ten o'clock curfew. How could my mother expect me to become an adult if I had to be home and in bed before the news was even on? So one night I succumbed to the temptation and formulated what I thought would be a Mama-proof plan. I plumped up half a dozen pillows beneath my covers, waited until my mother had retired to her bedroom, and then I silently tiptoed down the hall and out the door.

Miraculously enough, I made it home apparently undiscovered. But it wasn't until I was sitting at the breakfast table the next morning, bleary-eyed and exhausted, that I realized that Mama's rules might very well be for my own good. She wasn't trying to control my life as some authoritarian manipulator. No, she knew that a growing body needs rest and consistency more than the thrill of late-night foolishness. I'm sure I still had my moments of doubt and disobedience after that night, but I recall paying a little more attention to the motives behind my mother's rules and regulations. You see, I realized after my curfew caper that my mother was preparing me, not just to be a good son or a devout Christian, but for something much bigger. She was teaching me to be a student of life.

LESSON ONE

MAMAS TEACH US TO BELIEVE
IN GOD

Of all the life lessons my mama taught me, I can say without a doubt that one of her bedrock gifts to me was a living, breathing belief in our God. She did it with words, she did it with actions, with prayers and praises, with the way she responded to life's hardships and trials. She did it with the joyful gleam in her eye as she surveyed the beauty of His creation in the budding rosebush at the corner of our house. She taught me to believe in God when she knew I was watching her, and she taught me more powerfully on those rare occasions when she wasn't aware of my watchful eyes.

I count this as one of her greatest gifts to me because so much of life focuses on the power of belief. In fact, belief, if you ask me, just may be the greatest spiritual force that exists in all the world.

"Hmm," you may say. "What about love? Isn't love greater than belief?" Well, love is a great force, but love does little good for those who don't believe in it.

Okay, what about peace? "Isn't peace a great spiritual force?" you may ask. Yes, peace certainly does have a power of its own, but if people do not believe peace is possible, then peace never comes.

So much in our lives begins with believing — love, peace, growth, change, destiny — and I am so thankful that my mother always taught me to *believe.* She taught me to believe in God, which I want to elaborate on in this chapter, and she taught me to believe in myself, which I will address in the pages to come. The strong tide of my mama's many lessons flow out of the currents of these two streams.

I suppose my mother taught me to believe in God before she taught me to believe in anything else. She reinforced that lesson by taking my siblings and me to church every time the doors were open, by supporting and encouraging our church involvement, by teaching Sunday school.

More than those things, I saw my mother value God's Word in her own life, feeding her habit of personal prayer and looking to God for strength. She did not seek strength, wisdom, or comfort in other people, money, position, profession, education, or in the circumstances of life. No, she knew that people and situations change. Other human beings can greatly enrich our lives, but I think we would all admit that people do change. Some people are up one moment and down the next; they like you one day and hate you the next; they tell you one thing on Monday and then by Wednesday they have changed their minds. Not so with God.

The longer I live and the more people I encounter, the more I appreciate the fact that God does not change. He can be counted on. Hebrews 13:8 tells us that, "Jesus Christ is the same yesterday and today and forever." He does not have mood swings; He doesn't "evolve" in His thinking (because He has already attained the height of wisdom and understanding); He doesn't get angry and give us the silent treatment. Instead, God is stable; He's constant; He's *always* good, *always* right, *always* fair, *always* compassionate, *always* wise — and *always* there. He never, ever changes.

I know there are people who would challenge me. I can hear someone now asking, "How can you say God is always good when a tsunami wipes out thousands of people in an instant? When a hurricane destroys homes and lives? When a disaster like 9/11 devastates a nation in so many ways?" To those who are curious and those who are critical, my answer lies in the thoughts, experiences, and observations of the grueling hours and days immediately following the tragedy. Please allow me to explain.

I remember the magazine cover well: The question "Is This Man the Next Billy Graham?" floats in large letters next to a photograph in which I am holding a worn, well-used Bible. Because of the angle of the photo, the Bible appears as big as my broad shoulders. The corresponding article is a nice piece that highlights my preaching and notes the compassion that is demonstrated through our ministry. It mentions my love for and our ministry's outreach to those people who are hurting and gives a brief summary of my father's illness and death.

I appreciated the article content and approach, but I marveled at its timing. You see, this issue of *Time* magazine came out within one week of the September 11 attacks in 2001. It was on the newsstand as our nation suffered the most horrific acts of violence ever to hit American soil. Because of this timing, I was asked to make a number of television appearances to discuss, from a religious leader's point of view, the events we now call "9/11" and their impact on the soul of our country.

During the course of these interviews, I was often asked, "How can a loving God do such a thing?" and "How can a loving God allow such a thing?" My answer now is the same as it was then. God is a loving God indeed. In fact, He is so loving that He has given humankind the magnificent gift of free will. Yes, He has entrusted us with the power of choice. Without it, we would be reduced to robots. We would not enjoy the luxury of saying, "I prefer roses over lilies," or "I'll have the steak instead of the salmon," or "I would rather go to the beach than to the mountains." And when human beings are entrusted with the power to make their own decisions, then some people will choose evil over good. Some people will choose selfishly to the point that they will employ their human will to the destruction of others.

When such events happen, a loving God immediately begins to bring triumph out of tragedy. Those bent on devastating America were sorely disappointed. Every life lost left a gaping hole in the hearts of loved ones, but thankfully, the death toll did not reach the numbers that our enemies hoped for or that our authorities feared. In the wake of 9/11, unity arose in our nation — a wave of passionate patriotism swept our country from sea to shining sea, and we witnessed stunning displays of compassion and acts of heroism that took our breath away. Priorities were rearranged, relationships were restored, love was rekindled. We began to value our lives, our families, and our friends in fresh, new ways, and we decided not to postpone the pursuit of our dreams any longer. I believe that God was in these things.

We learned timeless lessons from that one day, and the lives of many Americans are better — more aware of the needs of others, more focused, more productive — because of it. I have grieved with and for those who lost people who were dear to them on September 11, 2001, but I have also seen great good arise from the bitter ashes of that day and I have thanked God that it was not any worse, even as I have wept and mourned for those who could not imagine anything ever being any worse. In the aftermath, I have seen God heal, strengthen, and restore a nation and its people. I know that He exists. I know that He loves. I am sorry for the choices some people make with their gift of free will, but I know that the God who gives it to us has done so out of love. Yes, I believe in God, not only because my mother taught me to believe in Him, but also because He has proven Himself to be real to me in more ways than I can count.

In fact, I know that I would believe in God even if my mother had not set me such a powerful example, because the thought of a life without faith is unbearable to me. Not long ago, a well-known talk show host commented during an interview that he would like to be able to believe in God and to believe in an afterlife. Having been a person of faith all my life, it really is hard for me to imagine living without believing in God. I cringe when I think about how my life would be if I did not believe in God. I really think the hopelessness, the meaninglessness, the loneliness, and the confusion would be too great for me to bear. If I did not believe in an afterlife, I would have been devastated by the loss of loved ones, I would be afraid of dying, and I would shudder at the thought that everything about me would be finished forever when my casket was closed.

I do not know about other people, but frankly, I find the demands of a busy life quite challenging, and I need God's help too much — and have received it too often — to believe He does not exist! On top of that, I have witnessed too many miracles — that cannot be attributed to a human ability or intellect — to believe He is not playing a role in everything that takes place in our world.

The summary of my belief in God is, first of all, that He does exist; second, that He loves everyone on earth and wants to help us in our lives; third, that He sent His Son Jesus Christ to die on the cross so that all of our sins could be forgiven; that the best news in the history of humanity is that Jesus defeated death by rising from the grave; and that by believing in Jesus' work, everyone can know God here on earth and enjoy eternal life when their journey here is complete.

While your mother may not have directly taught you to believe in God, it seems to me that the very fact that you have a mother is evidence of Him. Regardless of her faults and failures, she loved you enough to endure the excruciating pain of labor until you emerged from her body fresh into this world. If she abandoned you to others, either through adoption or into the care of extended family, as painful as that reality may be, it may also indicate her desire for you to have so much more than she could provide. Yes, even as our mothers may have failed us at times — after all, they are not perfect — they still are one of the first indications of the sovereignty of God in our lives.

Whether you had a saint for your mother or a woman swallowed by the harsh currents of life, or more likely a mother struggling in between, the lesson I would pass along to you about believing in God is: Believe. *Please,* believe. If you do not believe in God, I would ask you to give Him a chance. Put skepticism aside for a while and open your mind to the possibility that He is real and ask Him to prove it to you. Look into the greatest literary work of all time, the Bible, and read it as God's love letter to you. I challenge you to test its ancient words and principles, for they have been proven true for centuries. I believe God is real; I believe that He wants to be involved in your life. I believe that He can be trusted even when He cannot be understood. I believe that He is your biggest fan, your wisest counselor, your most dependable friend. And I believe that He is constantly working for your good.

Homework for the heart: What did you learn about God from your mother? How would you describe your belief in God at this point in your journey? What do you wish you could ask your mother about her relationship with God?

A mother's secret prayer: O Lord, You have given me this child to love and shepherd for You. Thank You for entrusting me as Your steward. Allow me to represent Your love and compassion in ways that would draw my children to know You and serve You. Amen.

LESSON TWO
MAMAS TEACH US TO BELIEVE IN OURSELVES

Chances are, you have just read the life lesson on believing in God and you may wonder whether I have changed my mind and now decided that believing in yourself is more important than believing in Him. Certainly not. I am not even on an equal par with, let alone greater than, the God of the universe — no one is. However, let me say that, as deep as my conviction is about the absolute necessity of believing in God, I value equally the fact that my mother also taught me to believe in myself.

One of the qualities I grew to appreciate in my mother over time was her sense of balance. She was not given to excess in any way (maybe that had to do with the Blackfoot Indian part of her ancestry), but she knew how to find the point of equilibrium between extremes and between opposites, and she knew how to keep a good thing from becoming an obsession. She kept our house clean but still found time to work outside the home, to spend time helping me with my homework, or to participate actively in our church. It wasn't as if she was a perfectionist, trying to be superwoman and juggle everything like she was the inspiration for Martha Stewart. No, she simply managed to be present in the midst of wherever she found herself, engaged by those around her, finely attuned to the leading of the Spirit and the timing of the Lord. Like the woman embodying wisdom in Proverbs 31 (more about her later), my mother managed to display remarkable agility in her ability to facilitate the many roles required of her.

Perhaps that is why I grew up not only knowing that God can do anything, but that I could do anything too. After all, the Bible says, "I can do all things through Christ who strengthens me" (Philippians 4:13). In fact, the empowering words of Philippians 4:13 were written by the Apostle Paul, a man who mocked and killed Christians before he himself had a life-changing encounter with God. He hated Jesus Christ — before he met Him. He had devoted his life to eliminating the spread of the Gospel — before the Gospel penetrated his heart. This man, who had so eloquently and violently attacked Jesus Christ, became one of the greatest servants of God in all of human history. He endured beatings, imprisonment, shipwreck, hunger, cold, persecution, and a multitude of other hardships because he deemed Jesus Christ worth suffering for. When we understand even this brief snapshot of Paul's life, we are amazed that he could say, "I can do all things through Christ who strengthens me." Paul's "all things" included trials and tribulations that leave our mouths hanging open and our eyes blinking in disbelief. If he could do all things, then you and I can do all things too.

Perhaps you're still skeptical. "It's all well and good for Paul to do all things, or for you, Bishop Jakes. But I'm just an ordinary person." Please understand that when I write about being able to do all things *through Christ,* I am not referring to a divine enablement reserved for the most holy people among us. I am talking about practical things that can be done by ordinary people. When God wants to accomplish something great or small, He uses a person. He does not sit in heaven on a throne and send thunderbolts and lightning strikes to make Himself known, as old-time Hollywood would have us believe. No, He works through people. I like to think of myself, and you too, as a pipe, and of God as the water. He is the substance; we are the delivery system. His power is expressed through our abilities.

Because God works through human vessels, many things happen — and I believe they are orchestrated by the enemy of our souls — to disintegrate our belief in ourselves. A broken pipe cannot carry water; all it can do is drip and leak. It is not good for anything, and in fact, it may cause damage. The same is true of broken people. They are not good conduits for God's power, they are not fit vessels for His use.

In order for people to be whole, strong, and able to help bring the desires of God to pass on earth, they must believe in themselves. They must resist the evils of self-pity, wounded hearts, rejection, and low self-esteem. Knowing how to stand up against these self-defeating foes needs to start in childhood. Growing up with a healthy estimation of one's self is much easier than developing it as an adult.

One way for parents to breed confidence in a child is to affirm and sharpen his thinking. Let me share an example. As a little boy, I talked all the time. I am telling you that my mouth went like a motor on a speedboat. I never gave my mother a moment's peace and quiet except when I was sleeping. Often, I made no sense whatsoever, but my mother always gave me her undivided attention. I could have been speaking Portuguese and she would have looked me in the eye and said, "Umhm. Really? I see. Oh, yes. That's good, son."

My mother's affirmation revealed her understanding of one of the great secrets of a person's development. She knew that my words revealed my thoughts, and that if *she* respected what I was thinking and saying, then *I* would respect my thoughts and words as well. Because she paid attention to me, because she dignified my mind and my mouth by focusing on me and entering into dialogue, she stimulated my thinking. The more she responded to me, the more I wanted to keep thinking, observing, learning, and sharing with her.

Of course, there came a time in my life when I did need to make sense. When my brain had developed to the point that I needed to be able to understand the conceptual and not just the concrete, and when I began facing issues that were gray instead of black and white, my mother was there, not only to pay attention to me, but also to help me grow in my thought processes. The more I could trust my own mind, she rightly surmised, the more confident I would be in myself.

You see, my mother knew from experience how important it is for people to believe in themselves. She had many obstacles to overcome and sadly, some of those obstacles existed because she was smarter, more diligent, or more ambitious than the people around her. When she faced jealousy or resentment, she let it bead up and roll off of her like raindrops off a freshly waxed car. She did not allow her critics the privilege of taking anything from her. Instead, she took their glances and their comments as fuel for the fire that burned within her.

Because I was taught to believe in myself, I am now doing things that were once just little dream seeds in my mind — not only preaching and pastoring a church, but also writing bestselling books, recording music projects, overseeing a record label, appearing on major television networks, writing plays, and even making movies. Many people with my background would not have attempted such pursuits, but I did — because I believed in myself.

Let me ask you: What would you do if you knew you could not fail? Now let me tell you that, as you develop more and more belief in yourself, you will arrive at the

conviction that you cannot fail. The fulfillment of your heart's desire lies in your ability to believe in yourself.

We are all responsible for believing in
ourselves. That is part of our job description as human beings. It is not anyone else's
responsibility to believe in you — and no
one else can do it better. Though people
can help you develop inner confidence, as
my mother did, no one can give it to you —
and no one can take it away.

To this day, I can recite lines from a poem
my mother taught me, words I have never
forgotten. It is a poem by Edgar A. Guest,
and a favorite of George Washington Carver,
who was an important leader at Tuskegee
Institute, where my mother went to college.
In these inspirational lines, this rhyming
inventor reminds us that we all begin our
lives with the same basic equipment and
that belief in ourselves causes us to rise
above the rest.

Equipment

Figure it out for yourself, my lad,
You've all that the greatest of men have
    had,
Two arms, two hands, two legs, two eyes,
And a brain to use if you would be wise,

With this equipment they all began,

So start for the top and say, "I can."
Look them over, the wise and the great,
They take their food from a common plate,
And similar knives and forks they use,
With similar laces they tie their shoes,
The world considers them brave and
    smart,
But you've all they had when they made

    their start.
You can triumph and come to skill,
You can be great, if you only will.
You're well equipped for what fight you
    choose,
You have legs and arms and a brain to
    use;
And the man who has risen great deeds
    to do

Began his life with no more than you.
You are the handicap you must face,
You are the one who must choose your
    place,
You must say where you want to go,
How much you will study the truth to know;
God has equipped you for life, but He

Lets you decide what you want to be.

Courage must come from the soul within,
The man must furnish the will to win.
So figure it out for yourself, my lad,
You were born with all that the great have
    had,
With your equipment they all began.
Get hold of yourself and say: "I can."

I cannot remember exactly how old I was when I learned to recite this poem as a young boy. The important thing is that I did. You see, a young person's self-confidence is a fragile commodity. It can be battered and bruised in the course of a school day if a bully says unkind words or if a teacher treats a child as though he or she is not as smart as the other students. It can be devastated on a basketball court or a baseball field if a child makes a mistake that costs his team a victory. It can be ruined at home if all a parent ever does is focus on the child's weaknesses and less-than-ideal qualities.

Most children could use someone to boost their self-confidence — someone to pat them on the back, to be there when they are performing, to cheer them on in their every endeavor, to encourage them to try again when they fail, and to applaud them when they succeed, even if their success is nothing more than a really good effort. Adults have enormous influence in the lives of their children, grandchildren, nieces, nephews, and young neighbors. I challenge you to be a great encourager of the children and teenagers who are part of your world, because the more you believe in them, the more they will believe in themselves.

People who do not believe in themselves do not get very far in life, and they seldom enjoy the progress they do make. A healthy sense of self-confidence can result in opportunities that might pass by a person with low self-esteem, and in accomplishments that the timid would not pursue. A confident person will attempt more, achieve more, and celebrate more than a person who is hesitant and full of self-doubt. I have learned by the examples of others, by experience in my own life, and by watching others as I have worked with people over the past thirty years that believing in ourselves is integral to success in every area of our lives.

Live the rest of your life believing mightily in yourself. A healthy sense of self-worth is invaluable and irreplaceable. Whatever it takes for you to believe in yourself more than you believe in anyone else on earth, do it. If you do not believe in yourself, others will not be inclined to believe in you either.

If you do believe in yourself, there is no limit to the greatness you can attain or the great things you can accomplish.

Homework for the heart: What did you learn about believing in yourself by your mother's example? By the way she interacted with you? What do you wish you had received more of from your mother? Why?

A mother's secret prayer: Dear God, thank You for the uniqueness of this precious gift that You have given me in my children. Help me to love them with Your love and to empower and equip them to be all that You have created them to be. Help my children to know how special they are to me, and to You. Amen.

SUBSTITUTE TEACHER
LEARNING FROM VIRGINIA
JAMISON

You may be wondering, "Who is Virginia Jamison?" Well, the short answer is that she was my mother-in-law. But she was oh so much more than that! Far from the usual attributes ascribed to the stereotypical mother-in-law, she was a great mix of tenderness and iron-hard strength. A no-nonsense, tell it like it is, rooting-tooting grandma who had a heart as soft as the inner lining of chitlins and hands as strong as a steel-mill worker, Mrs. Virginia Jamison was an amazing gift to me as a person. Before I ask my wife to reflect on her mother's life lessons, I must share a little of my own relationship with her.

My mother-in-law, "Mother" I called her (to distinguish her from my own, who will forever be "Mama"), was so different from my own mother — much quieter, less outspoken, a self-described "background person" who worked like a horse behind the scenes at my little church, but did not enjoy being put up front. Part of what made her so special is that she was gifted with the inner sense not to intrude on the marriage her daughter and I have shared for almost three decades. From the day Serita and I first said "I do," Mother supported us and nurtured us with the wisdom of Naomi in the Bible. When times were tough, she was a silent force. When times were good, she would smile wide and dance all over the church, as happy as a fat kid in a cookie-eating contest! What a gift she was to us!

Virginia Jamison was not a hat-wearing, shouting, praying phenomenon who dressed up but didn't get things done. No, her hands were always filled, first with one thing and then another. She was the president of the usher board, and she kept them as crisp and sharp as the military. She was also the president of the Pastor's Aide for most of my pastorate.

She was strongly supportive of my wife and me and she was the best grandma my children could have. My own mother never quite grasped the idea of taking care of kids who were not her own — maybe because raising us had worn her out! But my mother-in-law was the one who came down with food in the trunk of her car, shaking snow off her boots and coming in the house with everything imaginable to eat.

Now I have to be honest, not everyone liked her. Because although she was quiet, if you didn't do what she thought you ought to do as quickly as you ought to do it — well, she had no qualms about letting you have it. Yet somehow even her ability to be as sharp as a razor in a barbershop if you crossed her only added to her charm for me.

Maybe I loved her so madly because she loved me. You know, the best way to win anybody is to love them into submission. All I know is that, at the end of the day, I was so enthralled by her that I never minded her coming and going or staying around us. She was a cool breeze blowing beneath my wings when I was weary and tired. She always knew what to say and when to just listen and pray. She was not afraid to deliver a railing rebuke when appropriate, or to give her heart when needed just as quickly. She was a Christian, no doubt about that, but she was a Christian after the old African American church tradition. She didn't mind slipping back into where she came from if that was what she needed to do to get you straightened out.

I think what I miss most about her now

that she is gone is the simple fact that she was unpretentious, simply transparent without a need to camouflage who she was to impress anyone. She was that simple and straightforward in a world where you have to know people for years to really know them, and even then you are not sure that you have figured them out. When I met her, it was so refreshing to meet someone who wasn't trying to be more than she was, though she would never allow you to belittle her into a lesser role than she deemed appropriate, either.

When we lost her, we were all devastated. But as time has passed, I came to realize that I didn't really lose her at all. I found her in the hearts and faces of my children. Sometimes, they say or do something and I can swear I see my mother-in-law's deep-set eyes shining through their young faces. My wife, who grieved the worst at her mother's parting, doesn't even know that as she readies the girls for the prom, or drives wildly to get our son to football practice, she is becoming what she lost. Oddly, people die, but spirits never do. My mother-in-law is alive and well in all of those she loved and touched. Real mothers touch the world with grace and dignity, and my mother-in-law was no different. She surely touched me, and as my wife writes of her in the following pages, it is my prayer that she will touch you too.

MY MOTHER, VIRGINIA JAMISON
Serita Ann Jakes

She was a woman of the highest integrity and the deepest faith. She was a woman of quiet spirit and prayers that shook the halls of heaven. She was a woman of hidden strength and great transparency. She was such a hard worker, and she had to work so hard in order to make it. She was constant, unwavering, sober-minded, even as the shifting sands of life tried to make her lose her balance more than once. She was a woman of dignity and character, a woman who learned to govern her emotions while allowing her love to overflow.

There are not words rich enough or accolades high enough for my mother, Virginia Jamison. My best attempt to describe her would pale against the true definition of this amazing woman. And in order to better understand who she was, you would also have to know what she went through.

She was an only child, born June 19, 1926, in the small coal-mining community of Kimball, West Virginia. Both of her parents were present throughout her childhood and as she grew. When she married my father, James Edward Jamison, I am certain that her heart was filled with dreams of a happy home and a happy family. I am sure she never imagined the hardships that would come as my father tried to provide that happy home for us by working deep beneath the earth in the dark, dank coal mines of West Virginia.

I wonder when she realized that his cough was more than a regular cough, when she realized that his labored breathing could not be attributed to a stuffy nose or to the humidity that hung in the mountain air. I wonder how she kept her heart from breaking and how she faced with such courage and resolve the dreaded news that has devastated so many miners' families: black lung disease.

With my father's diagnosis came my mother's longest trial. We did not live near a hospital, so the entire burden of his care rested upon my mother. Hers was not only the heart that loved him, but hers were the hands that fed him and bathed him; hers was the voice that spoke strength to him when his own strength was clearly waning. And hers was the time and energy we children, my four siblings and I, needed in order to survive.

So for four years, my mother cared for her husband, making good on her promise to love him in sickness and in health. For four years, she cared for him, and only in the worst of times did she drive the snowy mountain roads to the hospital, where she sat beside his bed, gazing upon the shell of a man he became and at the tall, dark green oxygen tanks that kept him alive. At the same time, she was our provider, our breadwinner, and always, our mom.

My father's illness and subsequent death made it necessary for my mother to work, and she was faithful in her job as a housekeeper at the V.A. Hospital. She had health challenges of her own, but when she had exhausted all of her sick leave and all of her vacation time because of sickness, she simply had to keep working in order to support and care for the family.

I remember many Christmas mornings she could not be with us because she was working. But my mother always had goals; she always aspired to more than she currently enjoyed. As a result, she made time to take classes and develop new skills — and she eventually landed a job as a scheduling clerk. She was always well groomed, but what a joy it was for her to trade her housekeeping uniform for professional clothes!

I always knew my mother was on my side, that she was *for* me — and that she loved me unconditionally. She also loved me sacrificially and made perhaps the greatest sacrifice a mother can endure. When I was six months old, my mother realized that she could not care for me properly and that she could not handle the financial hardship of another mouth to feed. So she sent me to live with my aunt and uncle, about fifty miles away, because she knew they could provide a better life for me.

I lived with my father's sister, Aunt Ruth, and her husband until I was seventeen years old. My mother visited often, brought me gifts when she could, and always made a special effort to be present when I was being recognized for some sort of achievement at school or church. I stayed with her during the summertime and during holidays, but lived with my aunt and uncle during the school year for all twelve years of my schooling. I was never bitter toward my mother for not raising me as she wanted to because I always knew that she was making a tremendous sacrifice and only wanted what was best for me.

Aunt Ruth contributed to the frilly side of

me, the feminine part, the ribbons and bows. Her grown son lived in New York City by the time I went to live with her and he considered me his little sister. I loved opening the packages he sent me — dresses from Macy's, little lacy socks, and all the things little girls adore.

Aunt Ruth was protective. She didn't let me go beyond her yard to play, and seemed quite happy with the fact that I preferred reading to outside activities anyway. She discouraged any interest in boys, urging me instead to focus on my education. She was very domesticated, but never insisted that I follow suit. Instead, she allowed me to watch. I watched her keep a clean house; I watched her get up in the mornings before my uncle and prepare his breakfast; I watched her do everything a woman needs to do in order to run a household and be an excellent wife. And as I watched, I learned. Well, if the truth be told, the only thing I didn't learn to do was iron. When I introduced her to my future husband, she said to him in near horror, "Serita doesn't know how to iron and *you're a minister!*" He didn't seem to mind, and I quickly learned.

My years with Aunt Ruth were critical to my development. They taught me how to make a home and to be a wife and a mother

— an opportunity I would never have had at home because I did not get to watch my mother be a wife for very long before my father passed away. What I did see in my mother was a wife who kept her covenant, who honored her marriage vows, and upheld her promise "till death do us part." She taught me by example that loyalty and commitment to covenant are embedded in a person in very practical ways: when the going gets tough, you stay. She taught me that a husband and a wife go through everything together — and that's what makes their bond unbreakable.

Related to family life, my mother taught me to honor my father because of who he was on the inside, even when he became ill and unable to provide for us. Now, as an adult, I have taught my children to honor their father because of who he is on the inside, not because he has been granted a measure of fame and respect. My mother taught me to look at all people on the inside and to value them there. By the same token, she taught me to concentrate on building myself up on the inside. As a result, I grew up level-headed, rooted, balanced, and confident in who I am.

When I was older, the Lord gave me wonderful gifts of time with my mother. She was with me during the births of all of our children; we spent hours working at the church together; and she was my partner in art when I decorated my own home for the holidays. In fact, she was the one who hung out the window and made sure all the lights were blinking! She was with us for holidays and other gatherings, and she and I were privileged to be able to spend many special moments together.

One of the great blessings of my life has been that my mother and my husband held such deep respect for each other and were each so very fond of the other. As he and I struggled through our early years in ministry, we certainly depended on God, but as human beings go, she truly was the wind beneath our wings, the current on which we soared.

As my husband's ministry grew, we began to hear the Lord calling us away from our roots in the gentle mountains of West Virginia to the bustling metropolis of Dallas. Because my mother was such an important part of our ministry, we could not imagine making such a move and beginning a new work without her. So my husband went to her, told her about the move, and said to her, "Would you come with us?" She cried because she was so honored to be asked!

What courage it took for a woman past seventy years of age to pack up her home and leave the land she'd known and loved all of her life for a city she'd never seen, to minister among people she'd never met. But my mother was more than equal to the challenge. She embraced it, and when she arrived in Dallas, she got a house near the church so that she could easily help with anything we needed there.

Her move does sound remarkable and it was a remarkably generous thing to do, but you need to understand a bit more of her background in order to see that it was also quite a natural thing to do.

You see, my mother was a woman of great faith. She was a woman of the Word and a woman of prayer. She prayed every night on her knees (and I knew she was often praying for me). She had loved God all of her life, but to truly begin to understand her faith, you would have to know something about the furnace of affliction in which it was strengthened and refined. My father's illness and death took their toll on my mother. They taxed her physically, emotionally, mentally, and spiritually. But she came through that situation with grace and determination and with her devotion to the Lord intact. Then there came a year that held double tragedy for her. Within twelve months, she not only lost her own mother, but she lost her oldest son in a senseless act of murder. Her grief was deep, but God's grace was deeper still. That same year, she received the glorious baptism of the Holy Spirit, and the power of God was released within her in ways she had never experienced. Her devotion had never wavered in the face of her losses. She stayed strong, she stayed stable, she stayed with God and grew to know Him in ways she never had before. By the time she was asked to move to Dallas, she trusted Him completely. She knew that He does order our steps and that He gives us the ability to bear whatever we must bear. She did not need familiar surroundings; she only needed the presence of God. She knew if he was asking her to move so many miles away, that He would meet her there.

Something within her had always loved the church, honored her pastor (even though she always maintained her delightful individuality), and served God's people. She had sung in the choir at her Baptist church in West Virginia, she had been a member of the usher board, and she had been the one to decorate for banquets and other special occasions. (I got my love and gift for entertaining from her!) She instituted the first First Lady's Day (a day to honor the pastor's wife) in her church.

When my husband and I married, he was already pastoring. I have to admit that my mother was a bit concerned about my marrying a preacher, but it did not take her long to join our church and call her son-in-law "Pastor." From the very beginning, she acknowledged us as her pastors and was exceedingly faithful to our flock, even though she had to drive one hour to get there and one hour home, often through rain, snow, sleet, or hail. She was president of the Pastor's Aide, still caring for her pastor as she always had. She also sang in the choir at our church and served on the usher board, as had been her custom for so many years. When she retired, she did move close to the church. And, as I have already mentioned, when we moved to Dallas, she moved with us. That's just the kind of committed, faithful servant and loving mother she was.

At The Potter's House, "Mother" Jamison quickly won the hearts of everyone she met. She took on the responsibility for preparing communion, which was no small task for a congregation of thousands! She could also be found decorating for special occasions and banquets, as she had done for so many years. She also instituted First Lady's Day for me at The Potter's House, and I still smile with gratitude for her desire to honor me in that special way.

When my mother's time came to meet the Lord face to face, she suffered a stroke, was sick and hospitalized for one week, then died. I believe my mother was obedient to death. I believe that she realized that her condition would require a long and grueling recovery process — and she did not want to be a burden to her family. Even in death, she chose to put others first. She had always been so strong and so independent that when she knew her strength and independence would never fully function again, she simply allowed death to escort her into glory.

No one expected her to die. She was such a vital part of our family, such a vital part of our ministry, such a vital part of our lives. She was only seventy-two years old — and seventy-two years young. She was still able to drive her car, still serving God and His people, still loving life. I think she knew we were going to be okay. She had witnessed and participated in our lean years, but she had also seen God bless the ministry He had given us and she knew He was taking care of us.

On the day of her funeral, I could not get dressed. I was deep in grief, and deep in denial. She was such a servant. She was so strong. She was my hero. We buried her the week before Mother's Day. I could not bear to even acknowledge Mother's Day that year, but my husband told me that our children had planned something special for me and that I needed to participate. That Sunday, I noticed something I had never noticed before. I noticed how many people were wearing white roses, indicating that their mothers, like mine, had finished their course on earth. I realized that they had loved their mothers as I had loved mine — and that all of us have a responsibility to perpetuate the strength, the goodness, the wisdom, the character, and the faith we have learned from our mothers.

At times, I consider myself to have had two mamas — my mother and Aunt Ruth. Each woman deposited something rich and vital in my life, though the two of them were very different. Aunt Ruth was skilled at homemaking, and my mother could be considered "upwardly mobile" and professional. I am such a combination of these two women. I can stay at home and be happy baking cookies, but I can also stand with confidence upon a platform before tens of thousands of people or meet with dignitaries when that is required. Mother and Aunt Ruth were living epistles and, by reading them, I got what I needed in life. Their legacies live within me — and through me and the ministry God has given me, my "mothers" are now mothering all over the world.

LESSON THREE
MAMAS TEACH US TO BE
BROAD-MINDED

Of the many life lessons my mama taught me, perhaps none has allowed me to learn as much about life and other people as this one. Growing up in a time when it was so easy to judge a person by her skin color, her style of clothing, or her demeanor, my mother learned firsthand how to see beyond the cover into the real book inside.

Many people live fairly narrow lives. We exist in little boxes created by "our" people, "our" places, and "our" things. We crave the comfort of the familiar and often prefer what we know to what we have never seen. Leaving the comfort zones of our own neighborhoods and cities, our families and our institutions, our leanings and even our convictions is not always easy, but it is necessary if we are to grow as human beings. Just as a tall tree needs space to keep spreading its roots out underground so it can grow, so human beings need to keep

73

reaching beyond where they are so that they can develop to their fullest potential.

My mother knew this, and I have always been proud of the fact that she had a wonderful and very broad mind. I mean, that woman knew how to *think* — and she taught me to do the same. My mother did not have much patience for narrow-mindedness and was determined that neither she nor any of her children would ever be mentally small. She sacrificed in order to expose me to things she could not afford and to ensure that we would develop into well-rounded individuals with a variety of experiences. She exposed us to the ballet and the opera, to poetry and politics, to life's finer things and to the common, everyday things we simply needed to know.

In one of my attempts to exercise my own broad-mindedness as a young man, I visited a church where, well, let me just say that the people were very enthusiastic. I wanted my mother to see such passionate people, so I took her with me the next time I went. She was not impressed. I will never forget what she said after the service: "When you get through shouting, you still have to be somebody." Her point was that emotional expression might have been appropriate and acceptable within the walls of that church building, but that when the shouting was over, all of those people needed to be able to function in life. They needed to be able to use their minds, not just their mouths. They needed to experience a world beyond their own church because, for all of us, there is a world beyond the familiar.

People who are narrow have seen and experienced only one aspect of a whole and act like their one piece is all there is — and it is not. Sometimes this happens because of ignorance and sometimes it happens because of arrogance, but regardless of the reason, narrow-mindedness causes a person to live a very small and shallow life. People who are narrow-minded tend to be quick to judge and criticize others and to put themselves on a pedestal. They are unable to see the big picture in a situation, so they focus on the little things. Worst of all, they miss out on so many magnificent experiences they could enjoy if they would only open their minds.

There is a great big, wide, wonderful world beyond what most of us know and it's time for us to get acquainted with it. Let me encourage you to begin investigating and exploring music and theater, art and science, current events, history and literature, and everything else that composes the great symphony of the world in which we live. This kind of expansion of your mind will only serve to enrich your life. I know my mother's openness to all facets of life and culture certainly enriched mine.

My mother's broad mind had plenty of room devoted to great America writers, orators, and poets such as James Weldon Johnson and Walt Whitman. From time to time, I can still hear Johnson's lines lilting from her lips: "God of our weary years, / God of our silent tears, / Thou who has brought us thus far on the way; / Thou who has by Thy might / Led us into the light, / Keep us forever in the path, we pray." And I can hear her repeating with perfect cadence Whitman's mournful words: "O Captain! My Captain! our fearful trip is done; / The ship has weathered every rack, the prize we sought is won."

Through these verses and countless others, my mother's love of poetic wisdom was passed on to me. As I have pursued my own collection of favorite writers and poems, I encountered a verse from Henry Wadsworth Longfellow's *A Psalm of Life,* which eloquently and accurately describes the approach I believe we all need to take to living: "Not enjoyment, and not sorrow, / Is our destined end or way; / But to act, that each tomorrow / Find us farther than today." The only way we end up farther tomorrow than we are today is to increase our exposure and open our minds. We move along the path of life only as we experience new things, think new thoughts, entertain new ideas, meet new people, see new visions, dream new dreams, take new risks, and recognize new potential — and that means we need exposure to develop a broad mind.

While exposing ourselves to that which is new or unfamiliar is not easy, it's crucial if we are to grow and change into all that God intended. If we are truly going to birth the greatness that He has placed within us, then we must be willing to take risks and fly into unknown skies. I once preached a sermon series entitled *Seven Steps to a Turnaround,* to help people understand the practical aspects of the process of changing their lives. Step One is exactly the topic I am addressing here: exposure. I chose that as the first step to change because I know that without exposure, we do not grow. We stay stuck exactly where we are and we cannot make progress in life. A mind that never moves is like stagnant water; it eventually becomes ugly and begins to stink. A growing, changing, ever-broadening mind, though, is like a fresh, cool stream. Exposure to things that are new and different will challenge you, stimulate you, sharpen you, and expand your experience. It will also provide enjoyment and refreshment to you and to those around you.

Being broad-minded not only enriches our lives but, according to Scripture, it seems to go hand in hand with cultivating wisdom. The biblical King Solomon, often called "the wisest man who ever lived," wrote the book of Proverbs, which is loaded with nuggets of practical wisdom for everyday life. How did he get so wise? Writing about Solomon, the unknown author of the book of I Kings made the following observation: "And God gave Solomon exceptionally much wisdom and understanding, and breadth of mind like the sand of the seashore" (I Kings 4:29, AMP).

You and I may never achieve breadth of mind quite like the sand of the seashore, but that doesn't mean we shouldn't actively pursue it! I surely am! I encourage you — no, I urge you — to make a priority of pursuing broad-mindedness too. There is more to life than you may realize and your world is far larger than you may know. It's time for you to discover it. So, go to the opera; read a classic work of literature; learn a foreign language; take ballroom dancing lessons; go fly-fishing; figure out how to fix something; discover a part of the world you have never seen; expand your vocabulary; take a class at your local library, community center, or university; spend some time with older people and let them talk about how things used to be; attend a Saturday morning workshop at your local home improvement store; volunteer; read an international newspaper; trace your family genealogy as far back as you can go; study the stars; ride an elephant; learn to change the oil in your car; go to the symphony; invite someone you hardly know to dinner — just do *something* you have not done before! You will end up more well-rounded and your life will end up enriched if you will simply break your routine, discard the familiar, and explore ideas and experiences that are currently unknown to you.

Whatever strikes your fancy or piques your interest, explore it and encourage your children to do the same. Blow the sides off of the box you have been living in, and remember that exposure is necessary to progress in life. Go ahead. Take as many adventures of discovery as you can fit into your schedule, then block out time for some more. Take advantage of every opportunity you can find to discover and do something new. Invite others to join you, especially the young people in your life. Stretch your mind the way a sprinter stretches his hamstrings before a race. Find out just how much your thinking can be expanded. And whatever you do, as long as you live, do not stop broadening your horizons and opening your mind. Determine that your every tomorrow will find you farther than where you are today.

Homework for the heart: What did you learn from your mother about tolerating other people's differences? How did she foster your curiosity about all the amazing diversity our world has to offer? What did you teach your mother about being broad-minded?

A mother's secret prayer: Lord, I'm so grateful for the beauty and diversity of this amazing world that You have created and into which You have inserted me and my children. Thank You for creating so many unique individuals and interests. Open my mind that I might open my children's eyes to the wonder of Your glory manifest in our differences as well as our similarities.

LESSON FOUR
MAMAS TEACH US THE POWER OF WORDS

So many of our mothers taught us the life-changing impact that language can have on our lives. Probably like your mother, mine often corrected my speech when I used the wrong verb tense or slipped in the always forbidden "ain't." I recall once when, after such a correction, I replied, "Mama, I know the correct way to speak. It's just that I don't want to have to feel like I'm in English class whenever I talk to you." She looked at me for a moment with one of those looks that only mothers can muster — you know the one, where she raises one eyebrow and her lips betray the hint of a smile while her eyes reveal skepticism. She said, "Words are important, son. So important that you need to handle them with great care whenever you speak, write, or read." And she's right, proved out in fact by this very book, which is inspired by the impact her words of life had on me. Proved out as well by the words

82

I am privileged to speak from the pulpit or from the podium before thousands of people. Words have indeed shaped my life as well as my life's calling.

You may be saying, "That's fine for you, Bishop, but I'm not a pastor, speaker, or writer. Why should I handle words with care? How do they have such power?" Think about the way language is so essential to virtually every relationship, every profession, every endeavor. In fact, I am not sure that mental strength and intellectual sophistication ever achieve maximum potential and impact if the people who possess such knowledge cannot use words to convey the truths, facts, and ideas that are in their heads. Of course, society benefits greatly from the brilliance of scientists who record their findings more than they talk about them, from those who turn their knowledge into action in the forms of new medicines and new systems that serve the common good. But unless someone gets the word out about these advances, they do little good. Unless knowledge, experience, wisdom, and information are shared, especially through the spoken word, they fall short of their intended purpose.

Being an educator, my mother was not only aware of this truth but was devoted to sharing knowledge and wisdom, through the power of language, in the arena of her classrooms. And like most natural teachers, everywhere she went turned out to be a classroom with its own lessons just waiting to be discovered. I can remember her telling me that the whole world was a school and everyone in it was a teacher — and she admonished me to be sure I went to class every day. To this day, I respect people from all walks of life because I see them as having something that can help me grow and learn. I evolve in every conversation and transform in the midst of every friendship I have been blessed to experience.

My mother's intellectual abilities and accomplishments often found expression through her words. She would never have blurted out the things she knew or spoken in ways other people could not understand, but she spoke carefully, thoughtfully, intelligently, and appropriately in every situation. She was articulate, which means that she could put words to her thoughts, she could communicate effectively, she made her mouth the servant of her mind.

My mother enjoyed talking intelligently about what she knew. In fact, she was a member of the Delta sorority, and her association there provided her with many opportunities for public speaking. As a young boy, I often accompanied her on her speaking engagements and can remember being duly impressed with the dignified way she handled herself in front of a crowd and being so proud of her as she made beautifully crafted speeches. She was a poet on the platform, a skilled wielder of words — and I wanted to grow up to be the same.

One day when I was eight years old, following one of her speeches, I declared to her: "Right now they call me Mrs. Jakes's son, but one of these days they'll call you Tom Jakes's mother." I believed those words with all my heart — and they came true. By the time my mother passed away, people all over the world knew her as T. D. Jakes's mother — and I am proud that they did.

Even at a mere eight years of age, there was something in me that understood that being able to speak well was part of my destiny. I knew instinctively that I needed to learn to communicate — to develop my vocabulary, to learn to pronounce words correctly, and to learn to convey the thoughts in my head through the words of my mouth in ways that were clear and easy to understand. How did I know these things? How does any young person perceive his or her destiny? They just *know*. A person does not have to wait until he is grown to know his destiny. After all, Jesus Christ was only twelve years old when he spoke with such depth of knowledge that He astounded the priests and scholars in the temple. He just *knew;* many others throughout history have just *known;* and I did too.

Maybe my destiny was in my genes. Maybe my heritage had something to do with it. My mother was indeed an accomplished and gifted public speaker, but she was not the first in her family line. My mother's mother was probably a preacher — but people called her a missionary. (I think that was the term they used for female preachers in her day!)

The first time I remember seeing that saintly old woman, she was reading her Bible through her bifocals, with a quilt over her lap. As a boy, I exchanged letters with her, and when it came time to produce my first art project at church — a picture of Mary and Jesus — I carefully packaged it and proudly sent it to her. Though my grandmother has been gone for quite some time, her house remains in our family — and my childhood drawing remains in her house to this day. It's funny; even though I did not spend tremendous amounts of time with her, people who knew her tell me I sound just like she did. Imagine that.

Whether you come from a line of preachers and speakers, whether you are a naturally gifted speaker, or whether you must be diligent to hone your ability to use words well, let me encourage you to speak with passion and authority in an articulate way. Understand and experience how words can move people, how words can connect one person with an audience of thousands, how one person's words can reach another person's soul. Words are conveyors of hope, courage, and wisdom. King Solomon wrote that words are so powerful that "death and life are in the power of the tongue" (Proverbs 18:21). They can literally shift a person's entire life when they are well chosen and well spoken.

King Solomon also wrote that: "A word fitly spoken is like apples of gold in settings of silver" (Proverbs 25:11). *Fitly* in this context means "timely." So in other words, this verse is telling us that when we say the right thing at the right time, the result is of enormous value. You will rarely find a person or a situation in life that cannot benefit from apples of gold in settings of silver.

Toward the goal of speaking a word fitly, I want to address the mothers reading this book for a moment. It is important to know that the words you speak as a mother have power. I have seen those words build up a child like a soaring cathedral or tear him down to a pile of human rubble. I have seen them inspire or destroy development. Oh yes, I know that there are times you may feel that no one is listening. I am sure my mother would be shocked if she could read this book and realize that so much of who I am has been shaped by who she was. Similarly, someone you know and love is being shaped by what you say and do.

Let me ask you: How are you shaping your children as you speak to them? Are you like a potter, shaping the soft clay of your children's hearts with words as the potter crafts a vessel with a light, guiding hand at some times and with the gentle pressure at others? Or are you like a sculptor, using your words like the hammers, chisels, and knives because you are too busy and stressed to speak kindly and exercise patience?

When your children finish a conversation with you, do they look like fine pottery in the process of being molded by your words with love and care, or do they look like stone, having had parts of their hearts chipped away by negative, sharp, or angry words? If you are not satisfied with the answer, change the way you speak to them. Oddly, some mothers do not know that they can change the way they respond to situations. They feel helpless to change their words and actions, even though they later regret their outbursts.

You need to know that you do have the power to change. Your children will nurse at the breast of your wisdom and draw it out through your conversation. Make sure that this milk is free of contaminants like bitterness, envy, pettiness, or vulgarity. When you clean up your speech, you have partially cleaned up your act. Remember that one does not have to use profane language to curse someone. We can curse people with negative ideas about them. Mothers who say to their children, "You will never amount to anything" or "You will be ignorant just like your father" are speaking words that are curses. Perhaps one reason a curse carries such power is that it speaks to the end of the one to whom it's aimed. A curse suggests that the end is unsavory and doomed, that the person is beyond hope. So many children are doomed by curses that are unknowingly emitted from mothers, fathers, and even teachers at school. Instead of such a poisonous puddle, your mouth should be a fountain for cool waters of hope that spring fresh every day.

Be very careful what you say. Remember that death and life, blessing and cursing are in the power of your tongue. With the words of your mouth, you can impart greatness or smallness in someone else's life. You can fan the flame of a dream or you can snuff it out. Use your words for good!

Homework for the heart: What are some of your mother's favorite sayings? When would she say them? Why do they linger in your memory now? What did you learn about the power of language from your mother? How has she influenced the ways you speak and write?

A mother's secret prayer: Dear Lord, thank you for the gift of Your Word and the incredible power of language and communication. I pray that I might use my words with care and teach my children the impact that our words can have on our lives. May I only use words to build up my children, to comfort and heal, to instruct and inform, never to tear down or impair. May my children use the words of their mouths and the letters on their pages toward this same goal of loving others as You love us. Amen.

LESSON FIVE

MAMAS TEACH US TO BE RESPONSIBLE

It has been said that children learn from what they see. If that is true, and I believe that it is, then I was watching a living visual aid by observing the way my mother endured hardship. Little did she know that some of my greatest lessons came from watching her not complain or whine when the task was tough, even when she wanted to quit.

As I was growing up, perhaps the foremost lesson I learned from watching her was to be responsible. I suppose I knew what the word "responsibility" meant long before I knew how to spell it! I knew that it meant doing what I said I would do, keeping my word, admitting my mistakes, making right a wrong I had inflicted, apologizing when needed, using common sense, being honest, and taking serious things seriously. Part of my learning came from my mother's own character and convictions — and part of it came from sheer necessity.

You see, my brother is seven years my senior and my sister is five and a half years older than I am. They had already left home during my late childhood and teenage years, and my father was ill. Since he was unable to work, my mother had to have a full-time job. Thankfully, it was a good job with the Equal Employment Opportunity Office for the state of West Virginia. With my siblings away from home and my father unable to do much, I was the only person my mother could count on, so I had to be responsible. If the truth be known, there really was no room to be irresponsible because her expectations would not allow that. Honest to goodness, I thought she would kill me if I didn't do what I was supposed to do!

While my mother consistently demonstrated it before me, she talked to me about the importance of responsibility before she ever entrusted me with it. By the time she gave me something to be responsible for, I knew I had better not mess up! I can well remember her sending me downtown in the city where we lived with the instruction to mail a letter, deliver a message, or pay a bill. She taught me to do business with various merchants in town, and even gave me checks to write once I was old enough to do that.

In addition, I was responsible for several household chores and, of course, for my schoolwork. But the most serious responsibility of all involved my ailing father. He became ill when I was about eleven years old, and his health deteriorated for five agonizing years before his once-strapping body slowly succumbed to the daily death of kidney disease. While he was sick, he needed to be fed; he needed to be shaved; he needed to be kept clean; and he needed someone to meet some basic medical needs. After school, while other boys were riding bicycles, shooting basketballs, and roaming in the West Virginia hills, I was cleaning up a sick room. I was trying to put a smile on a dying man's face. Other boys were, for the most part, carefree. I was responsible.

Lest you think I begrudge my young friends and neighbors, let me hasten to say that I do not, not in the least. I am simply reporting the realities and the differences between our lives in those days. Looking back now, I am glad I had to learn to be responsible. It has served me well all of my life — and it will do the same for you. It has made me honest and trustworthy, hard-working and confident. It has offered me the courage to embrace visions that seemed too much to handle. It has taught me to take seriously my role and visibility as a public figure and to balance the many demands of my life. It has enabled me to guard the trust that has been placed in me by God, by the people in my family, my congregation, and my broader audience. It has given me experience I might not have otherwise had and enabled me to achieve goals I might not have otherwise attained. I can enjoy many fruits of life today because I learned to be responsible at an early age.

The importance of this lesson does not emerge simply from the rewards that being responsible affords. This lesson is doubly important because refusing to wear the mantle of responsibility — a garment that I believe fits us better each year as we practice this virtue — leaves us and those around us naked and cold. You see, I simply cannot just extol the benefits of being responsible; I must also warn you of the dangers of not being responsible.

Irresponsible people — be they men or women — do not keep their word; they cannot be trusted. They are as elusive as the proverbial greased pig in a room full of butter, always slipping and sliding away from commitments and relationships that require them to stand firm. They will not be where they say they will be when they say they will be there, if they ever show up at all. They will laugh, cry, scream, or pout at inappropriate times in order to make themselves the center of attention, even if it means disrespecting others and ignoring their needs. Irresponsible people will have a long list of excuses for any need that might arise. They will always blame somebody else. They seek shortcuts wherever possible. They do not respect authority. They are masters of the "spin," often beginning sentences with, "Well, it wasn't really like *that* . . ." or "What *really* happened was . . ." or, "No, baby, you don't understand . . ."

Simply put, irresponsibility leads to low living. It spirals into shortsightedness and immediate gratification and often ends in drunk driving and debt and unemployment. It keeps people from developing the God-given potential that is within them and locks them in a prison of self-doubt and self-hatred. It produces children who are not loved. It brings heartache in countless ways — for the irresponsible person and for others. It ruins a person's health and renders a bright future impossible.

On the other hand, being responsible positions a person for increase. To those who are faithful in small things, much more will be given. For example, a person who is responsible in financial matters can be trusted with more money. A person who manages his time well can handle more opportunities. Someone who is responsible in his profession will be in line for promotion.

The more you learn to accept responsibility, the more success, enjoyment, and confidence you will have in life. I believe that there is a world of potential within you. I believe that there are dreams waiting to be fulfilled, personal and professional goals waiting to be reached, adventures waiting to be embarked upon. In order to make and maintain progress in any of these areas, you will have to take responsibility for some things — and I know you can.

Let me encourage you once more to embrace the responsibilities that are yours. Do not shy away from responsibility, for it is a key to your growth. If you have not taken responsibility for your life, your thoughts, your words, your actions, and your future, I am asking you to start today. If you do, the quality of your life and the depth of your faith will only increase.

Furthermore, I challenge you to help develop the ability to handle responsibility in your children. You do this by starting small — telling them to make their beds every morning or to put their shoes in the closet when they take them off. You move on to telling them that they need to set their own alarm clocks and be responsible for getting up on time to be at school by the time the bell rings. When they begin to drive or to go out with friends on the weekends, you set a curfew by which they must be home.

As your children grow from infancy into adulthood, you will naturally give them different types of responsibilities, appropriate to their age and season of life. A five-year-old cannot be expected to handle the same responsibilities as a teenager. What is important is that responsibilities increase as the child grows and that you are consistent in your expectations and in doling out consequences for irresponsibility. If these things sound harsh to you, I need to tell you that they are not; they are simply the means by which you help a person learn to be responsible. A five-year-old who has to skip her favorite cartoon because she did not make her bed one week will learn to make that bed before her show airs again the following week. A fifteen-year-old who must relinquish her iPod for a week because she "forgot" to study for the big science exam might well remember the date of her next important test. Better yet, when she is twenty-five, she will have learned that irresponsibility has a price, and her history of learning to manage responsibility will position her for the ever-increasing responsibilities that accompany adulthood.

Perhaps you feel challenged to teach your children how to be responsible when you're still learning yourself. Don't worry — remaining humble and admitting our mistakes is part of being responsible! You see, there is no ignoring it. Responsibility will either build a person's muscles or illuminate his weaknesses. Embracing responsibility will produce a great leader, while dodging it will result in a person who lags far behind others and may not even be a good follower.

Accept — no, *own* — the responsibilities that belong to you. Do not run from them, for being responsible is a pathway to becoming successful. It prepares us to do more, handle more, overcome more, experience more, and succeed more than those who are not willing to accept responsibility. Opportunities to be responsible present themselves to all of us, often in the form of adversity. When trouble knocks on your door, stand up to it. We often have to be the caretakers of difficulty — and that will develop our ability to handle responsibility like nothing else. Learning to take responsibility will bring maturity and integrity to your life and in the lives of your children in ways nothing else will, while maturity and integrity will pave the way for a life of fulfilled dreams, peace of mind, and great success.

Homework for the heart: Would you describe yourself as a responsible person? Why or why not? What did you learn about being responsible from the way your mother conducted herself and her duties? In what ways do you wish your mother had been more responsible? Why? How can you improve on yourself in these areas?

A mother's secret prayer: Oh, God, thank You for the gift of free will that You have entrusted to us, Your children. I ask that I take full responsibility for all that You have entrusted to me and that I pass along a similar sense of stewardship to my children and all that You entrust to them. Allow us to work hard as Your loving servants and to trust the rest to You and Your sovereignty. Amen.

SUBSTITUTE TEACHER
LEARNING FROM CORETTA SCOTT KING

In the early 1960s, the Kings' name was in the mouth of every then-called Negro in America. My family was no different. I can recall my father listening intently as Dr. King delivered his address in the profound style of oratorical grandeur that is classic to his name alone. My mother, who had stopped doing what she was doing to join my father at the family black-and-white TV set, mentioned with resonating pride, "I went to school with Mrs. King."

All of us children asked excitedly, "What?" My mother's comment meant that she was semi-famous — almost, sort of, and in a way.

She continued, "We sang in the choir together at Lincoln High School."

I later learned that Mrs. King had a beautiful voice, so I was not surprised that she had been a chorister in her younger days. Years later, I would meet Bernice, daughter of Dr. and Mrs. King, and strike up a conversation in which I mentioned that our mothers attended school together. After swapping stories about Marion, Alabama, and childhood experiences, we left with a deep and abiding mutual respect for each other, bound by the continued legacy of our parents' emphasis on excellence, pride, and inner strength. My parents were far less notable than Bernice's, but equally as committed, and had instilled in me a deep respect for the King family that continues to this day.

I will never forget several years ago when we dedicated our new sanctuary at The Potter's House. The Dallas Symphony Orchestra served us that day and the crowd was arrayed in the regalia typical of a church congregation on such a celebratory occasion. Our then governor, George W. Bush, was invited but unable to attend, and he sent greetings and congratulations. Among those who were able to attend were notable names like the then vice president Al Gore, Rev. Pat Robertson, Rev. James Robinson, and many others whose names brought great applause from the crowd. But when I presented Mrs. King to the crowd with her daughters, Yolanda and Bernice, in tow beside her, the crowd went wild! The beautiful piece of artwork that was presented to me that day remains on my desk even now, years later, and captures a memorable moment that is irreplaceable to me. On various occasions thereafter, Martin III, Yolanda, and Bernice have all been guests at our church.

Down through the years, I entertained both Mrs. King and most of her family. I was also a guest at her birthday party a few years ago and, more recently, was privileged to be in her home for lunch while visiting in Atlanta. This woman, who traveled with presidents and yet had the grace to understand paupers, embodied in her persona a distinct reality of an era of black pride and courage that we will likely not see in the same way again. She was the guest of countless groups of all colors and classes. She traveled throughout Africa and was well respected by people like former president Nelson Mandela and a host of other distinguished people. I was so impressed with her that she was the recipient of our Women of Purpose Award during MegaFest 2005.

While waiting on lunch to be prepared the day I visited her at home, Mrs. King shared many interesting stories about her life with Dr. King, stories that will inspire me and enrich me all of my life.

As African Americans, we shared Mrs. King with her family, in a sense, but I know from raising my own children that healthy and understandable proprietary feeling the children of highly visible people have about their own families. There is nothing as rich as the inner circle of a family whose huddle has been the necessary shield to protect them from the harsh winds of public scrutiny and the bright glare of overexposure. I will cautiously avoid the temptation to take the liberty and say that Mrs. King was my mama too. Instead, I will yield to her daughter, the Reverend Bernice King.

In the following pages, she speaks to us not so much as a woman of God or public figure herself, but as a daughter who can help us understand how her mother did what she did and give us clues as to how she held her family together when life tried to pull them apart. Eavesdrop with me as Bernice shares her perspectives on the great influence of her mother and the impact she felt from being up close and personal with a woman whose class and social grace made her the queen of the black community.

MY MOTHER, CORETTA SCOTT KING
Bernice King

"How is Daddy going to eat now?" I wondered aloud as my five-year-old mind pondered the difficult reality that my father had been killed. Actually, I was told that he had "gone to live with God," and was concerned about how he would be fed, since he was no longer living with us. My mother answered by saying something like, "God will take care of that." She then wrapped her arms around me, pulled me close to her, and told me, "Mommy loves you." With the profound wisdom of a mother who can discern her child's true curiosities and fears, she was addressing a need I didn't even know I had. In those three words, she let me know that I was safe, that I was deeply cared for, and that I would somehow be okay in the wake of my father's assassination.

My mother, Coretta Scott King, never wanted the kind of life that would leave her a widow at the age of forty-one. She would not have chosen the path she walked — the path of a pioneer, the path of a true change agent, the path of freedom and justice for all. Nevertheless, she was destined and divinely prepared for it. She gave dignity to a difficult situation and showed amazing strength of soul when the soul of our nation was torn apart; she demonstrated unspeakable courage when fear threatened to paralyze so many people; and she never wavered in her convictions, despite fierce criticism, rejection, tragedy, and loss.

What makes a woman as brave, as steadfast, as committed to a cause as my mother was for more than half a century? What makes a woman willing to suffer and even to die for an ideal? What compelled her all those years? What enabled this mama to make a difference not only in my life, but in the life and values of an entire nation and the world? I suppose we need to begin answering these questions by looking back to a small town called Marion, Alabama, and take a peek at my mother's beginnings.

She made her appearance in the world on April 27, 1927, and spent her childhood amid the grief and horror of America's Great Depression. Like many youngsters of her day, she was acquainted with hard work from an early age. Where she lived, "hard work" often took the form of picking cotton — and by any standards, it was hard work indeed! Sometimes people do not realize what grueling labor it is — how the sharp ends of the bolls can rip the skin on a person's fingertips, how heavy a sack of cotton can get on a person's back, how stifling and filthy cotton fields can be. But under the enormous weight of her task in the field, amid the swelter and the sweat, my mother's character was crafted, her spiritual and emotional strength forged, her discipline developed, and her perseverance produced. She learned in the cotton fields not only to endure through tough situations, but also to overcome. She was known to pick more cotton than her male cousins!

Even though the Depression robbed many people of their dreams and caused many to compromise their values, my mother had been born into a family in which education was important to women — even though the women in her family had to overcome the two towering obstacles of being black and being female — and they were not willing to sacrifice that, even though money was scarce. As a young girl, she and other African American students walked several miles each way to her school — while the white children rode the school bus. When she was older, she studied at a boarding school called Lincoln High School. Even though a boarding-school education was expensive, her mother insisted upon this type of education, even if she (my grandmother) only had one dress! She knew the power of education to make a difference in a person's life and in the world, so my grandmother prioritized schooling even over something to wear! After high school graduation, my mother continued defying cultural norms and the odds that were against her by virtue of her race and gender. She attended and was graduated from Antioch College in Yellow Springs, Ohio, just as her mother and sister had. The words of the college's first president, Horace Mann, resonated within her: "Be ashamed to die until you have won some victory for humanity." My mother's intellectual path was not typical, but it was necessary for her. It was part of God's will for her, part of His destiny for her life — even though she had no idea how that destiny would unfold.

After college graduation, my mother moved to Boston to attend the New England Conservatory of Music and fulfill her dreams of becoming a classical concert singer and a music teacher. One day in 1952, she was introduced to a man named Martin Luther King, Jr., who was pursuing his Ph.D. at Boston University. Two destinies linked arms, two destinies that would later converge to change a nation — but my mother did not know it at the time. Although Martin was intelligent and had a charismatic personality, my mother was not romantically interested in him at all. He was too short, she thought, and she certainly did not want to marry a preacher! She knew that her calling in life was to make a difference in the world, and she felt destined to change the condition of blacks in the South, but she felt that her contribution would be through music, not through ministry.

As my parents became acquainted with each other, they discovered that they shared similar concerns about the plight of African Americans in the South. They saw how differently their people were treated in the North, and they longed for the South to migrate north when it came to the opinions and treatment of African Americans. My mother was always a champion of hope, dignity, and freedom; she was never one to tolerate violence or injustice. She was involved in the peace movement prior to meeting my father. As such, she was one of the first to persuade him to speak out against the Vietnam war.

Even though my mother was not initially attracted to my father, she did sense that there was something different about him. She may not have imagined or understood the magnitude of his influence, but she knew in her heart that he had what it took to rise above ordinary men, to lead others and to make the world a better place by his thoughts, words, and actions. The call to destiny that she heard in her soul became louder and clearer when she connected with the vision, the zeal, and the convictions in my father. Ultimately, I believe it was her deep internal recognition of his greatness that enabled her to put aside her dreams of changing the world through music in order to join him and adjust to his way of advancing the cause of a better life for every African American in the United States. However, she did use her training in voice and music education through Freedom Concerts that were designed to educate people about the movement, as well as to raise funds for the movement.

Of course, God knew all along that these two revolutionaries would end up together, and they were perfect for each other. My mother was tailor-made for her situation and when God created her, He put within her everything she would need for the life she was called to live. She is a real-life example of Jeremiah 1:5, which says: "Before I formed you in the womb, I knew you; before you were born I sanctified you."

God helped my mother along in His plans for her life by giving her a dream that confirmed to her she was to marry my father. She became his wife in June 1953 and they chose to return to the South for

111

my father to begin his pastoral career. Though he had job offers in the North, they both felt a pull to that region of the United States where slavery had once been the societal norm and where their own people were still treated as less significant, less valuable, indeed less human than their white counterparts. My parents were change agents, and the South was where change was needed. Their passion was to make a difference, to have a lasting positive impact on a society that was so unjust — and he knew that the pulpit would provide an excellent platform from which to champion God's ideals — equality, Christian love, liberation from social and economic oppression, and peaceful resolution to conflict.

My mother was not naive. She knew that a life dedicated to societal reformation would not be easy — that it would be full of conflict and controversy; that it would be lonely; that it could be dangerous or even tragic. She had seen glimpses of the opposition to change that existed in the South, especially where blacks were concerned. Perhaps she got her pioneering spirit and courage from her father, who had been viciously threatened because he was the first black person in the community to own his own business. But he was tenacious and unafraid, even when forced to look down the barrel of a white man's gun. He always said to my mother: "Look a white man dead in his eyes and he cannot do anything to you." That's what my parents did; they looked the disgrace of inequality square in the face.

Aware of the difficult road that lay before them, my parents did return to the South in 1954, after my father completed his doctoral dissertation and agreed to serve as pastor of the Dexter Avenue Baptist Church in Montgomery, Alabama. Little did my parents know, when they moved there, how significant this city would become in their lives and in the life of our country.

My mother was a wife of uncommon maturity and strength. She was never one to nag my father, to want or cause him to worry about her well-being, to call his attention to things at home, or to say to him, "But what about us?" Instead, she was extremely encouraging to him and submitted to the destiny and call that was upon their lives. She did everything she possibly could to be supportive of the cause and to make sure that she was okay so that she would not be a distraction to my father. She always knew something could happen to her, but never said, "Martin, back off." She never allowed fear to dictate her commitment to the movement, and she was willing to make personal sacrifices for it. She knew that she and my father were doing God's will and she was totally yielded to that.

My father received threats too numerous to mention and through them all, my mother just kept right on living. She didn't bow to a single one. A specific threat did become reality one day after a particular group informed my father that they would blow up his house (my parents lived in a parsonage at that time) if he did not leave town in three days. Unintimidated, of course my parents did not leave — and the house was bombed, with my mother and infant sister inside. They survived.

When the bombing occurred, my father was preaching at a nearby church. He rushed home when he received the news and found an angry mob of black citizens surrounding the house. After he learned that my mother was safe and amazingly calm, he walked onto the porch to address the enraged crowd. He instructed them to compose themselves, to put down their weapons and to fight with Christian love instead of with guns, knives, sticks, and words that worsen a situation instead of defusing it.

As you might expect, my mother's father

was alarmed when he heard about the bombing. The night of the bombing, my parents stayed at the home of some friends, where they heard a knock on the door in the early hours of the following morning. It was my grandfather, who had driven from Marion, Alabama, to get my mother. He told her, "I've come to take you and the baby back to Marion." She responded with incredible bravery: "No, Dad, I'm going to stay here with Martin." And stay she did — through the sit-ins, the boycotts, the jailings, the marches, the speeches, the media frenzy, the heartbreak, the anger, the persecution, the violence, and the ultimate sacrifice of the man she loved.

After John F. Kennedy was assassinated in November 1963, my father often said that he would die the same way. He was always willing to die for his beliefs and he knew that his earthly life would most likely come to a violent end because of his convictions and someone else's intolerance. Several weeks before my father was killed, he had sent my mother some artificial roses so that she would always have flowers from him.

Likewise, my mother also knew in her heart that he could be killed someday. She lived every day fully aware of the cost of the cause — and fully aware that she might one day have to go on without her husband and to raise my brothers, my sister, and me alone. My father had always wanted to identify as much as possible with "the people" and to sacrifice all he could for the movement, so it was never important to him for us to own a home. My mother, however, knew intuitively that she and her children would need a place to live after my father's inevitable death, so she wisely convinced him in 1966 to buy the house we were renting at the time. That was the house I grew up in and the house where she lived until August 2004.

Until her death, my mother was strong, steadfast, and courageous. She was a woman of extraordinary character and, as I have already written, extreme maturity. She was a woman of honesty and integrity, of forgiveness and grace and love for others — and she imparted these values to me. She did not have a public persona and a private persona because she "walked her talk." She did not speak of her convictions publicly while failing to honor them privately, but displayed them when she was in the spotlight and when she was not. Looking back on all she endured, I marvel at the way she lived her life, a life of true godliness, which is so rare. One of the things she said — and

116

I saw her live it — was: "I don't hold grudges." So true. My mother obeyed the biblical command to forgive. She could have easily become a very bitter, angry woman, but she did not. Instead, she seldom spoke about her critics and refused to seek revenge or engage in "tit-for-tat" situations. She did have human feelings, but she didn't reside in them. She went on.

And so, my mother's legacy will also go on. Part of her legacy, of course, was to secure my father's legacy in the world. There were people who hoped she would disappear from the public scene after his death and stay home to take care of us children. But I like to say that she raised four children while she helped to raise a nation. She became more visible than ever as she sought and fought to open the King Center, which is the official living memorial to my father, and to work for my father's birthday to be observed as a federal holiday. Each January, the holiday not only causes us to honor my father, it also focuses the collective conscience of our nation on the ideals — especially the Christian ideal of nonviolence — for which he stood. The holiday also reminds us that, without those ideals, we would be no different than any other war-torn, blood-soaked nation on earth. Her efforts have called a country to remember that a peaceful approach to conflict is forever embedded in our history and woven through the fabric of our national life.

My mother made an incalculable difference in my life, in our family, in the United States, and around the world. Chances are, whether you realize it or not, she made a difference in your life too. If you love freedom and fairness, if you appreciate the value of other people, if you believe in peace and in the potential of every human being — then my inheritance is your inheritance. You have received what my mother most dearly loved to give.

LESSON SIX

MAMAS TEACH US TO PRAY

My mother was a woman of faith and conviction. She definitely helped to secure my belief in God. But she was not a sweet, sappy, super-spiritual saint who carried her Bible everywhere she went and greeted people with "Praise the Lord." No, she was a real person with real challenges — and she had a real faith in a real God. She had a relationship with Him in the deepest part of her being. It was like bedrock beneath every obstacle she ever faced, every emotion she ever felt, every decision she ever made, and every victory she ever gained. She did not flaunt it, she did not spiritualize it, she simply lived it.

In teaching me to pray, my mother never sat me down at the kitchen table and said, "Now, son, this is how you pray. First you say this and then you say that . . ." No, she taught me through exposure. Now, many of us may have been exposed to prayer in various contexts throughout our lives. We have heard people pray in our churches, and in our schools if we are of a certain age. We may have grown up in a family that paused before mealtimes to thank God for our food. We may have seen people pray on television as we watched state funerals or events such as a presidential inauguration. We may have found ourselves in situations so desperate that we have uttered almost a primal cry to God for help or relief. Then again, we may be people who live by prayer, having plumbed the depths of relationship with God through the communion of prayer. Nevertheless, like a first kiss from a secret crush, we never forget our first awareness of what it means to converse with God.

My own exposure began around the table. I suppose that is where I first became aware that people talk to God. Of course, growing up in church, I heard people pray in my Sunday school classes and in church services. At times those prayers stirred my soul and at times I did not really understand them. I did, though, believe God was listening and I knew that He could answer. But there came a point when my exposure to prayer solidified into a concrete commitment to heavenly communication.

My sister became sick. In her early twenties, she was diagnosed with a brain tumor. It was a gut-wrenching, heartbreaking situation, one our family could do nothing about. Of course, we could feed her and take care of her and ensure that she received the best medical care we could find, but at the core of the matter, we were powerless to heal her. We were helpless when it came to being able to ease her pain or relieve her symptoms. All we could do was pray. My family's prayers became urgent, fervent, passionate, desperate, and unceasing, as they went forth from our house with the speed, focus, and force of a steady stream of bullets aimed at the throne of God. My mother led the charge.

And let me tell you, nobody can pray like a mama whose baby is deathly ill — even when her baby is an adult. I had never heard anybody pray the way my mother prayed when my sister was sick. I had heard plenty of people pray, but never like *that*. She would not back down, she would not let down, she would not calm down. She would not get up and she would not shut up as she literally bombarded heaven on my sister's behalf. She became a warrior far superior to any epic hero. She became a giant on her knees. With a sword in one hand she battled the enemies of death and disease, and with her other hand stretched toward heaven she kept beseeching God's help and His mercy.

Have you ever heard the sound of desperation in another person's voice? I heard it during those days. I am sure the halls of heaven shook with the force of her intercession. She meant business — and she knew how to do business — with God. Though my mother's prayers were intense and emotional at times, they were not based on emotion; they were based on faith. Her passionate pleas were built on her deep and intimate acquaintance with God, her years of relationship with Him, her knowledge of His Word. She knew who He was, she knew what He could do, she knew what He had promised — and she went to war for those things to come to pass in my sister's life.

"What happened?" you ask. Let me just say that today my sister is a strong, healthy, beautiful mother and grandmother. She had an excellent education and a distinguished career in her profession. She has authored books, she is a public speaker, she is a delight to our family, and she is a trophy and a testimony to the power of prayer.

The Bible says in James 5:16, "The effectual, fervent prayer of a righteous man avails much." My mother was a righteous woman and she prayed "effectual, fervent" prayers. God heard and answered her, just as He will hear and answer you. Lest you be discouraged, let me hasten to say that being a righteous man or woman is not difficult. It is not earned; it is received. And it comes to all who embrace Jesus Christ as Lord and Savior. Your prayers can be effective if you will pray them fervently and out of the sincerity of your heart.

God loves prayer that comes from the heart; He treasures and honors real prayer. He wants to hear from real people who are fully aware of their deep and desperate need for Him. He does not have much regard for prayers prayed to impress other people or for pray-ers who are more concerned about the rhythm or the eloquence of their words than about the content of their plea. In fact, Jesus Christ had some choice words for such people and some clear instructions about the attitude we should have when we pray:

And when you pray, you shall not be like the hypocrites. For they love to pray standing in the synagogues and on the corners of the streets, that they may be seen by men. Assuredly, I say to you, they have their reward. But you, when you pray, go into your room, and when you have shut your door, pray to your Father who is in the secret place; and your Father who sees in secret will reward you openly. And when you pray, do not use vain repetitions as the heathen do. For they think that they will be heard for their many words. Therefore do not be like them. For your Father knows the things you have need of before you ask Him. (Matthew 6:5–8)

My life, like yours, has included its thrills and its chills, its sweet victories and its bitter defeats, its overwhelming challenges and its experiences that seemed greased with grace to accomplish. I have been told things that put a smile on my face and a laugh in my belly, and I have been told things that were so painful I had to remind myself to breathe. I have had moments when nothing seemed to fit and moments when everything has come together. I have pastored a church with only seven members and a church with more than thirty thousand. Through everything — I mean, through it *all* — I have prayed. I pray publicly, of course (preachers do that), but I pray like a madman in private.

I know that it is not the eloquence of my words or the volume of my voice that catches God's attention. It is the fact that I know I need Him. His ears perk up at the passion and sincerity of my heart, not at the poetic quality of my prayers. The same is true for you.

You see, prayer serves as a rudder by which we steer our life's course. It often works just beneath the surface of our lives. We need not desire for anybody to know it is there or to prove that we are doing it; we simply need to make sure that it rides along with us as an integral part of our lives.

The seas on which you sail may be stormy at times. There will likely be days when the chilly winds of life blow so hard that you will surely veer off course if you cannot pray. Your voyage, at times, may be lonely, but through prayer you will find a Companion, an ever-present Help, a Captain who always has the time and great desire to listen to you and respond with wisdom far beyond what mere men possess.

Like so many other lessons, I believe prayer is best taught by example, and I encourage you to begin passing along a prayer legacy to your children if you have not already started. A child who sees and hears you pray will learn to pray in his or her own way. You can provide guidance by encouraging children to pray before meals, when they have a test to take at school, when someone is sick, or when their feelings are hurt. You can remind them to thank God when prayers are answered. The point is to help them realize that they are not alone in life and that they can appeal to a source of help beyond their parents or any other human being. They need to know that God loves them, cares about them, wants to be involved in their lives, is cheering for them, has a great plan for their future, knows best, can be trusted, and loves to hear their voices. Teach them to talk to Him often. Tell them that they need not bow their heads, close their eyes, and fold their hands in order to be heard, but that they can commune with the Maker of the universe in the privacy of their own souls. Let them know that if they will only turn their thoughts toward God, He will listen and respond.

There will always be situations and circumstances that you cannot change for yourself or for your children. There will always be something over which you are utterly powerless — and it may be something potentially devastating. In such moments of crisis, there is no substitute for prayer and there is no source of strength and comfort like prayer. I am reminded of a line from an old song I have known for years: "King Jesus is a-listening when you pray." Let your voice be heard in heaven — and let me assure you that God is listening when you pray.

Homework for the heart: When did you hear your mother pray? On what occasion would she talk to God? What did she teach you about prayer and communicating with Him? How does this affect the way you pray today? What would you like to tell God that you've been reluctant to say to Him? I encourage you to open your heart to Him and listen for His voice.

A mother's secret prayer: King Jesus, thank You for always listening when I pray. Thank You for speaking to my heart and to the hearts and ears of my children. May we be attuned to the voice of Your Spirit and committed to the chorus of honest communication that You, our Master, modeled with Your Father. Help us to know that God is never too busy to listen and respond to us, His children. Amen.

LESSON SEVEN

MAMAS TEACH US TO LET
GOD BE GOD

Now you've already seen that two of my mother's most important life lessons center on God (although all her lessons come back to Him in some way, which is not surprising, considering her vibrant faith). Yes, believing in Him is important and learning to pray without ceasing is crucial. Without these two cornerstones in place, it truly is impossible to know the peace and joy of fulfilling the destiny for which you were created. However, there's another lesson my mother taught me related to God that was one of the hardest to learn. Simply put, I had to learn to let God be God.

One of the first occasions where this lesson emerged was in the aftermath of a winter snowstorm. Walking down the hill below our house, I became annoyed at the way my mother held my hand so firmly, restraining me from romping in the glorious white powder layered around us like blankets of spun cotton. I strained and pulled, tugged and tossed until finally my mother gently released her firm clasp of my hand. Turned loose, I proceeded to bound toward an especially high snow drift when I fell flat on my butt! The cold stung my body with its penetrating icy power infiltrating my prone body. Mama smiled in a knowing way, making it unnecessary for her to say, "I told you so!"

I thought I did not need to hold my mother's hand, thought that I knew more than she did about how much freedom I could handle. But what I learned is that I was not as adept at walking through the storm as I thought I was. I needed the security of an anchor, a mainstay in the slippery terrain beneath my feet. Similarly, in adulthood I've learned that so often I think I know what I should do and how I should do it. I tell God where I'm going and what I'll be doing when I get there. He must smile to Himself, much the same way my mother grinned that day in the snowy hills of West Virginia. He knows that I don't hold on to Him; He holds on to me.

And He holds on to you as well. It's so tempting to become arrogant as we grow and mature, to directly or covertly believe "we can do it my way, God." Instead of waiting out the storm, allowing the ice to thaw and reveal His path, we trudge ahead in our headstrong freedom until we fall flat on our faces and wonder what hit us. Usually, it's our own pride and arrogant nature that's chilled us with our fragility and fallibility.

There's another mother who also teaches us this lesson of letting God be God. She was barely more than a baby herself, a young teenager, perhaps. In her ancient culture girls embarked upon their journeys of marriage and motherhood much earlier than many do today, and she was already engaged. She definitely had marriage on her mind, but motherhood? Eventually, yes, I am sure, but not before the wedding. It has been said that the best-laid plans of mice and men often go awry. Young Mary was neither mouse nor man, but her plans were nonetheless challenged by a God who has a way of intervening at the least — or at times, I think, interfering — with what we have planned. Such was the case for her.

We know her as Mary, the mother of Jesus. The mention of her name makes us think of purity, holiness, dedication to God, surrender, and much later, the greatest agony a mother's heart can endure. What can today's mothers learn from her? I think that the greatest lesson a woman can gain from everything the Bible teaches about Mary's life is this: let God be God. Of course, I realize that God is God and that no person on earth has the power or ability to "allow" God to be God. But, when it comes to His working in and through a human life, a person can cooperate or resist. God has to be Lord and not just Savior to each of us. He needs the uncontested, irrevocable right to alter the course of our lives to accomplish His will in and through us. This is not about Christ the dictator, who forces His will on unsuspecting, defenseless victims. No, he is a gentle God, who allows us to choose whether we will comply with His plan or seek our own. I have done both. I kid you not. I have done it His way and I have done it my way. I humbly confess that His way is far superior to my own. Let me ask you today: Do you submit or are you in a state of conscious or unconscious rebellion?

Mary chose to cooperate with God, and in this chapter, I want us to explore together her humble response to His big surprise in her life. Consider what happened to her. I suspect she was in many ways an ordinary girl in Nazareth. She had given her heart to the young carpenter, Joseph, and looked forward to becoming his wife. Preparations were under way for a Jewish wedding and, if she was like many other brides-to-be, she went about her daily work with a song on her lips and a spring in her step.

Then one day, an angel appeared to her. He was not an ordinary angel, but an archangel, the angel Gabriel — one who stood in the very presence of God in heaven and came to earth on special assignment from the King of kings. One might think such a mighty heavenly being would visit a ruler of nations or a wealthy, prominent landowner. But no, Gabriel came to see Mary, the unassuming young woman who had no idea that she was destined to give birth to the Son of God. Gabriel's visit certainly changed Mary's plans and brought a divine interruption that would change not only her life, but the lives of untold millions throughout human history.

Gabriel's greeting was perfect: "Rejoice, highly favored one, the Lord is with you; blessed are you among women!" (Luke 1:28). Of course, Mary was startled, even "troubled," the Bible says. But the angel quickly sought to put her at ease in His holy presence. "Do not be afraid, Mary," he said, "for you have found favor with God" (Luke 1:30).

I want to stop here for a moment and

make sure that you know something today: you have found favor with God. You are not much different from Mary; you are highly favored of God. I have come to learn that favor does not always seem favorable at the time. Mary had received favor at one of the most difficult times in her life. She was being discussed all over Bethlehem and it was not favorable. Her beau was praying feverishly about whether to divorce her. Now, that was not favorable. In her day, separating once a couple had announced their engagement required divorce. Can you imagine, the groom wants a divorce because the bride is mysteriously pregnant? Now, that does not sound like favor either. Sometimes favor looks and sounds more like trouble and disparity. But be not deceived, there is often a great deal of favor hidden in unfavorable events, events that cause the soul to grimace and the heart to ache.

Knowing that God has chosen us for a blessing is not difficult to accept. It is when we realize that favor often shows up in unfavorable moments of life that we are afraid to proceed with that unalterable "yes" that God longs to hear us say to Him. Have you ever been afraid to be in the will of God? I know about being afraid to be out of the will, but sometimes it is frightening to do what God says to do even when you know it was He who told you to do it.

Even with Gabriel's declaration of God's favor to Mary, she still found herself afraid, as I suppose any young lady would. I would imagine that a supernatural gentleness and peace were infused in the angel's words when he told her not to be afraid. You see, when we are afraid, we cannot perceive God's plans clearly. Fear causes us to run from His purposes instead of embracing them. Our fears must be dealt with if we are going to fulfill the destiny God has placed upon our lives. If the grip of fear is holding you back right now, hindering you from enjoying your life and from doing what God created you to do, then hear the words of the angel: "Do not be afraid."

Easier said than done, I know. I do not think I have ever met anyone with enough strength to evict fear from his or her heart. But God is able to do it in an instant. Tell Him that you do not want to be afraid another minute, and ask Him to make you strong and courageous. He will delight to do that for you. Most of my life, I have been afraid of what He had in mind for my life. Even the great blessings were intimidating. Sometimes trusting God is horrifying, especially when you realize that God is not given to discussing details or getting your permission before He gets you in a compromising situation. Mary was just walking along and here came God into her life with a life-changing, plan-altering revelation. Ever been there? I have. I am not a woman and I certainly know nothing about carrying a child, but I do know what it is like to carry a ministry, a business, a family, and many other things that disfigured me, often got me into a rough test, and threatened to destroy me or my name along the way. What do you do? I say you feel the fear and do it anyway. The way to ensure ultimate success is to resist the fear and pray against it, but get busy doing what you have been directed to do.

Once Gabriel had acknowledged and addressed Mary's fear, he began to speak God's message to her, the best news ever announced on earth at that point: "And behold, you will conceive in your womb and bring forth a Son, and shall call His name JESUS. He will be great, and will be called the Son of the Highest; and the Lord God will give Him the throne of His father David. And He will reign over the house of Jacob forever, and of His kingdom there will be no end" (Luke 1:31–33).

Apparently, Mary adjusted quickly to the

destiny that had been proclaimed. She did not accuse the angel of being crazy, she did not challenge his words, she simply said, essentially, "Okay. Great. I can accept that all of this is going to happen, but I just have one question. You see, I am a virgin, so how is this going to work?" It was a reasonable query, given the biological requirements of human reproduction.

Gabriel explained: "The Holy Spirit will come upon you, and the power of the Highest will overshadow you; therefore, also, that Holy One who is to be born will be called the Son of God" (Luke 1:35). In other words, "Mary, this is not normal. This is of God. It's going to happen supernaturally. God Himself will place His seed within you by the power of the Holy Spirit." Is it not strange that sometimes God's plans sound so unusual that you cannot find anyone in whom you can confide? You know that if you were to tell people that God wants you to open the business, start the church, or undertake some other endeavor with no means of supporting your dream, they would be skeptical, to say the least. God's plan to bless you may not come with a support system. It may be controversial, and the only way to sustain yourself may be to find someone who has been there too.

No wonder Mary walked in Elizabeth's house and gave her a big salutation. When no one believes what God has told you and you finally find someone with whom you can relate, you will naturally be thankful for the fellowship in the struggle. Have you ever wished you had someone to talk to, someone who has been through what you are facing right now? I have good news. For every Mary, there is an Elizabeth somewhere, waiting on the doorbell to ring. Get up and find your Elizabeth and ring her bell. She has things to tell you that will strengthen you on your journey. Mary would not have to walk her miracle path alone. How compassionate of the Lord.

Then, Gabriel utters the words that have echoed in human hearts throughout history, words that have strengthened the weak and emboldened the fearful, words that have been light in the darkest of situations, words people have clung to when they had nothing else: "For with God nothing will be impossible."

I want us to pause again here before we proceed with Mary's story. Read these words again: "For with God nothing will be impossible." Whatever you are facing today is *not* impossible. Healing is not impossible. Deliverance is not impossible. Getting the job you need is not impossible. Seeing your child drug-free is not impossible. Graduating from college when you are fifty years old is not impossible. Paying off that debt is not impossible. A happy marriage is not impossible. No matter what you are up against or how difficult it appears, it is not impossible with God.

Years after Gabriel proclaimed that nothing is impossible with God, Jesus Himself spoke similar words to a father who had almost given up hope for his son's deliverance. He said: "If you can believe, all things are possible to him who believes" (Mark 9:23). Notice that Jesus said, "If you can believe." Is anything in your life holding back your ability to believe? Have you become discouraged, disappointed, or depressed about a circumstance or situation? Has a series of events siphoned the faith out of you?

I have come to speak an encouraging word through this printed page to you today. I have come to fan the embers of faith that may be smoldering in your heart. I have come to blow a fresh wind upon those coals that want to burst into a flame of faith, but need a little help. I have come to declare to you with the living and active word of God which says that all things are possible to him who believes, that nothing is impossible with God. I am asking God to give you a fresh impartation of faith for what seems impossible, and I want you to ask Him too. He will not let you down!

Once you really grasp the truth that nothing is impossible with God, I hope that you will respond as Mary did: "Behold the maidservant of the Lord! Let it be to me according to your word" (Luke 1:38). Once we believe that nothing is impossible with God, we can relax. That's really what Mary did; her response might be phrased in modern language like this: "Okay. I'm yours, Lord. Do whatever you want with me."

Mary's willingness to cooperate with God's plan for her life meant having to tell Joseph she was pregnant, knowing he would know that her baby was not his. She risked losing this man she loved, her friends, and her reputation as a devout Jewish girl. She made herself the subject of whispers and gasps all over Nazareth. All of these things, and the countless other hardships and embarrassments she certainly endured, took immense courage. Maybe she thought through the ramifications of saying, "Let it be to me according to your word," and maybe she did not. We do not know whether she was one to weigh the consequences of her decisions or whether she was a more spontaneous type of girl who simply said yes to God on impulse. We do know that she submitted herself to His will. Why? Probably because she believed that nothing is impossible with Him and that the rewards that come from Him are far greater than anything her obedience could cost her.

Do you have the courage to walk through a season of disfavor, knowing that it will lead to a greater manifestation of God's favor in your life? I hope your heart will echo Mary's and that you will say to the Lord, as Mary said to Gabriel, "Let it be to me according to your word." I know that God has an amazing plan for your life, but He will not force it on you. You, like Mary, must trust Him enough to say, "Let it be." And then, as He did for her, He will do something through you so fulfilling and so astounding that you can hardly wait to say, "Do it again, God!"

We need to understand that it is one thing — a wonderful thing — to submit to God's plan; it is quite another to walk out that plan one step at a time. That is where we find the grace that follows obedience. Mary's journey was not easy. We have already considered the public shame she must have felt as an unwed expectant mother in her culture. Thankfully, God informed Joseph about the matter through a dream, so he did not abandon Mary in her time of need. No, he was faithful and caring as they awaited the arrival of God's Son.

The only problem was that Joseph had to travel — right when Mary's baby was due — from Nazareth to Bethlehem for the rough equivalent of a census. The two of them made the trip, and while they were there, Jesus was born.

She did not give birth in a palace or a military hospital, as mothers of kings often do, but in somebody's smelly stable. She did not place Him in a golden cradle, but in a manger lined with straw. She did not wrap Him in royal robes, but in ordinary swaddling clothes. I wonder sometimes if the simplicity of it all surprised her. After all, she knew He was the Son of God. You are not the first mother who did not have what she felt she needed. But God sends the Messiah in a manger to remind us that conditions do not have to be favorable for us to produce effective and favorable results.

Mary's journey into motherhood began, I believe, the moment "the power of the Highest" overshadowed her. It took a quantum leap forward in Bethlehem's humble stable. Scripture does not allow us to see the details of Mary's mothering. We do not know how she related to the Son of God as a screaming infant or a curious toddler, aside from the fact that Jesus and his parents were separated in a crowd in Jerusalem when He was twelve years old and that Mary and Joseph found Him three days later, sitting among the teachers in the temple, listening to them and asking them questions (see Luke 2:46).

We do know that Mary's son, Jesus, fulfilled the great purpose for which He was born — the redemption of the entire human race. Because His mother submitted to God's call, embraced the interruption of her own plans, and allowed God to be God in her life, salvation is available to us today. Had Mary refused, God would have found someone else, for He was determined to save His people. But she did not — and that has given her a unique place of honor in human hearts and in human history for centuries.

Homework for the heart: Recall a time when your mother allowed you to do something on your own when she really wanted to help you. What did you learn from the experience? How often do you allow God to be God in your life presently?

A mother's secret prayer: Dear God, please help me to yield myself to You just as Mary so willingly served You. You know so much better than I do the paths that I should follow and the turns along the way. Especially along this journey of mothering, I pray that I would trust You and demonstrate to my children that You alone are the only One who can be God. Amen.

■ ■ ■ ■

PART TWO
BIOLOGY LAB:
LESSONS ON LOVE
FROM OUR GREATEST
TEACHERS

■ ■ ■ ■

So many women discover that the man they marry often sees qualities of his mother in his wife. And it certainly makes sense that we men look for women who model the positive attributes of our mothers, since Mama was the first one to hold us, comfort us, nurture us, encourage us, and demonstrate what it means to love someone.

Interestingly enough, many men often meet and marry a woman "just like Mom," only to find that they feel pulled in different directions more than a wishbone at Thanksgiving dinner! They want to "leave and cleave" and be united with their wives. But they also want to honor the woman who loves them more unconditionally than any other. Perhaps a certain amount of this triangulated tension is only natural. For instance, a mother naturally wants to see her children and their families at the holidays. A wife may naturally want to spend it with her parents or staying home and making distinct family memories of her own.

It's the wise mother who knows when to step back or when to step forward in her children's lives, especially after they become adults. It takes a wise mother indeed to teach her children how to love over a lifetime, to learn the give and take, the tightrope of relationships and responsibilities, commitments and communication. According to some mothers with whom I've been privileged to speak, teaching your children how to give — and receive — love may be a mother's most important job.

This lesson came to the forefront of my relationship with my wife when we were still dating and not yet engaged. I brought her home to meet Mama, nervous and desperately praying that they would both at least respond favorably to each other, this one woman who had given me life and the other with whom I was just beginning a new life. The meeting went well, with each woman liking the other as they embarked on this new journey of relationship bound by their mutual love for me, the man whose heart they shared. Afterward, when I returned from taking Serita home, I asked my mother what she thought and told her that I was going to marry this young woman that she had just met. Mama said, "That's good, son, really good. She loves you." I paused for a moment and said, "I love her." My mother looked at me and said, "You may love her — in fact, I know you wouldn't be thinking about marrying someone unless you did — but she loves you. It's important to know that you're going to receive love as well as give it to the person with whom you're going to spend your life. Remember that God first loved us."

Mama's words have stayed with me and become a tool of wisdom that I pass along to my children as they venture out into the laboratory of love known as dating, that place where hearts are laid bare and dissected by dedication. With my daughters in particular, I have told them repeatedly to never go first! It's hard to resist being captivated by someone who loves you and risks giving you their heart before you have given them your own. Falling in love is relatively easy. But catching the love offered by another is much more difficult.

This is but one of the lessons learned by looking at the intricacies of the heart in this unique laboratory of human relationships, risk, and romance. Join me now as we venture forward with a variety of mothers as our teachers and learn more of what it truly means to love and to be loved, not just with those we date or marry, but in the variety of relationships we are privileged to experience.

LESSON EIGHT

MAMAS TEACH US TO HIDE THEM IN THE HOUSE

I grew up on a dead-end street at the top of a mountain in rural West Virginia. Our little yard comprised a ten-by-twelve-foot area and included some sparse patches of grass and one lone tree that stood like a sentinel guarding our modest castle. While I liked our little yard and could use my imagination to turn it into a pirate ship or the Wild West, I longed for the greener pastures of the local recreation center, where I knew all the other kids my age seemed to congregate, playing basketball in the gym or chasing each other in impromptu games of freeze tag. Yet no matter how many times I asked or how desperately I pleaded, my mother insisted that I remain in our little yard within her eyesight. She wanted me in the yard or in the house, not out in the world.

I didn't understand her rationale at the time, and looking back later in life as a young adult, I felt confused. For you see, after the age of twelve or so, my mother was very generous in granting me the freedom to come and go as I pleased. In fact, she often sent me on errands for her into town. How could she have gone from being the jail warden to the great emancipator in such a short period of time?

It wasn't until later in my adulthood that I realized how she came to trust releasing me out into the world because she had supervised and nurtured me throughout my childhood. She made sure that I learned what it meant to be obedient and responsible, to be innocent and intentional, before she turned me loose.

There's something about loving someone, particularly our children, that compels us to hide them in our hearts, to safeguard them against the brutal realities of the world for as long as we can. But we know that no matter how much we love someone, we cannot protect them and shelter them forever, for clinging too tightly only hinders their growth. Still, we can prepare them, can give them time to grow in strength and stature so that when the time comes for them to venture forth, they will have a confidence and a firm foundation upon which to build. Mothers in particular seem to have a special sense about how long to allow their children to be children and when to push them gently from the nest so that they may fly on their own wings.

While I certainly experienced such a process, I am by no means the best example. No, to find the perfect poster boy for this lesson of love we need to examine the life of one of the greatest historical figures of all time, a man named Moses. This Old Testament hero's life began under the threat of death. He made plenty of mistakes as he grew and matured, but he evolved into a strong and wise leader of the nation of Israel. When God declared that His people, the Hebrew children, had had enough of the bondage and oppression of their slavery in Egypt, Moses was the man appointed to stand up to the mighty Pharaoh and lead the people out of captivity toward a land of freedom and blessing.

Lest you be tempted to think that Moses' job was easy or glorious, let me remind you that the people he led, even though they were called God's special ones, were prone to murmur and complain, to be greedy, to be impatient, and to give up on God when they grew tired and weary. Yes, those Israelites were a handful, to say the least, but Moses proved equal to the challenge of being their leader. Though he himself was not allowed to enter the Promised Land, he managed to position an entire nation to take possession of it and to get them through formidable challenges to the point that they were ready to fight for it. He trained his successor to lead the battle charge into that place of milk and honey, and died knowing that a new generation would possess the promises he had heard from God decades earlier. When he passed away, God Himself reached down from heaven and buried him. I cannot imagine a greater honor.

You know as well as I do that successful leaders do not just emerge on the scene of a nation. Men and women of Moses' ilk are not overnight wonders. No, they are the result of a lifetime of preparation, wise counsel, good decisions, and hard work. Most of the time, too, they had someone in their lives who recognized the greatness inside of them, someone who knew that, with the right training, these people could arise to positions of influence and excellence.

Being able to recognize the future voice of authority in an infant's whimper requires a special gift. Being able to see that the toddler who waddles across the living-room floor will one day stand before kings and princes takes an unusual amount of discernment and vision. Realizing that the little girl who follows you around everywhere you go has what it takes to lead a nation demands an eye that can look at what is and see what can be. Then, once parents accept that their children are destined for great things, they must know how to guard and guide those young lives so that the seeds of greatness will burst into full bloom in the right way at precisely the right time.

I believe that Moses' mother, Jochebed, knew her baby son was born to accomplish a mighty task. She certainly wanted him to have the opportunity, or she would not have gone to the trouble of waterproofing a basket and floating him in the river. The Bible tells the story this way:

> And a man of the house of Levi went and took as wife a daughter of Levi. So the woman conceived and bore a son. And when she saw that he was a beautiful child, she hid him three months. But when she could no longer hide him, she took an ark of bulrushes for him, daubed it with asphalt and pitch, put the child in it, and laid it in the reeds by the river's bank. (Exodus 2:1–3)

Why did Jochebed need to hide little Moses?

Well, Moses was born in Egypt, while the Israelites were working as slaves. Pharaoh had ordered the midwives to kill all baby boys born to Hebrew families. He had noticed that the more the Hebrews were afflicted, "the more they multiplied and grew" (Exodus 1:12). He was afraid that the sons of this ever-strengthening people would grow up to form a mighty army against him and that they would overtake his government. The way to avoid and evade that, he reasoned, was to kill them as soon as they were born.

Against this threatening backdrop, Moses entered the world. How did his mother manage to birth him safely into such horrific hostility? We cannot say whether she was attended by merciful midwives who let her baby live or whether she had no midwife at all. We simply know that Moses survived and that Jochebed was determined for him to live a long, full life.

I want you to notice that Jochebed "hid him three months." This one woman defied an edict of the king and outsmarted the government soldiers by keeping Moses hidden. We can only imagine how frightened she must have been, how fervently she must have prayed that he would not cry or need a diaper change at an inappropriate moment, how she must have had to put away his tiny clothes or little playthings every time she heard a knock at her door.

No, hiding her baby could not have been easy. But something inside Jochebed knew that the challenges, the inconveniences, and constant fear were worth it. She knew that she had given birth to a life worth saving — and in order to save him, she had to hide him. By hiding him, she ensured the eventual deliverance of her nation from slavery. She hid, as a baby, the man who would hear God speak from a burning bush, who would command the Red Sea to part, who would receive the Ten Commandments, who would write the first five books of the Bible, and be called God's friend.

After three months, hiding Moses in the house became either impossible or unwise. At that point, still bent on protecting and preserving his life, she put him in a basket daubed with asphalt and pitch to keep the water out and laid him among the reeds along the riverbank. She could not have known what would happen to him. She did what had to be done, even though it must have broken her heart, in order to keep him alive. I can almost hear the words that must have darted through her mind that day: "There's greatness in this baby boy. He's

157

got a purpose to fulfill. Don't let him die. There's greatness in this baby boy . . ."

You know the rest of the story. Pharaoh's daughter rescued Moses from his tiny ark and raised him as her own son. When he was older, he killed an Egyptian man and then hid himself for years in a place called Midian for fear of retribution. But when God called him out of hiding to rise up and become a great deliverer, he answered. He did not always display great courage, he did not handle every situation well, but he accomplished the task he was destined to perform.

The wise and courageous Jochebed knew a secret that would serve today's mothers well. She knew how to recognize greatness and she knew that greatness needs to be hidden at certain times. She knew that a child of destiny cannot be treated as ordinary, cannot go along with the demands of culture — otherwise, Moses would have been dead before he was a day old.

You realize, of course, that when I write about greatness and destiny, I really believe that such seeds are in every child. I believe your children are living, breathing bundles of incredible potential and that their potential is enormous. And, when I write about "hiding them in the house" I do not mean literally confining children to the four walls of your home. I do not mean sheltering them to the point that they are not able to function as smart, reasonable human beings in a complex world. (That is called "dysfunction.")

Hiding them simply means that you do not allow them to be exposed to everything that others may encounter. Now I know this is not easy to do, as they have access to much adverse information. Hiding normally is something that is born out of fear, but in this case we are talking about hiding them out of faith in God, faith that He has some higher purpose that will require them to be uncontaminated. That means that when you know God is going to use your child, you must teach him or her that fitting in is not as important as remaining conscious of your destiny and purpose. It means saying to your child, "You don't get to do what the others are doing," not out of fear or cruelty, but out of wisdom and courage and an interest in that child's future. My mother would say that being a good mother is not always about being friends with your children! You have a job to do as a parent and your goal is to get them ready for greatness with as few distractions and deterrents as possible.

Sometimes that means that a child has to stay home and study when others are at a rock concert. Sometimes it may mean visiting a grandparent in a nursing home when friends are watching a movie. It may mean practicing a musical instrument or an athletic move while others are playing video games. It may mean getting up early on Saturday morning to go to work while others are sleeping. All of these exercises in diligence — and others — do pay off. Your children may complain, but they may not see in themselves what you see in them. While they are under your care, the burden of responsibility is on you to help them develop their potential. You must do this wisely, careful to discipline them without breaking them and to build their self-esteem without giving them reason to be arrogant.

It takes courage to hide your child when every other mother you know is putting her children on display. It takes discipline to keep the hope-filled secrets you know in your heart about your child. I assure you, though, your difficult choices will be rewarded. There are rewards for good mothering. When you see the results of your courage, your wisdom, and your stewardship of the greatness that was entrusted to you in your children, your heart will soar. Hang in there, my sister, because payday is coming!

You remember that Jochebed hid Moses in the house for three months and then had to put him in the river. Along your journey as a mother, you will reach various points where you cannot continue to do things the way you have always done them. Your heart will remain constant, but your methods will have to change. This may include the way you speak to your children, the way you discipline them, your expectations of them, the "rules of the house," the way you express your love, or the way you show support. There will be times when you must change your strategy, when you must turn your thoughts from how to keep the baby quiet in the house to how to keep him dry in a floating basket.

There will also come a day when the best thing you can do is release your grip and let your child go. A mother needs to know when it is time for a transition. You will have to walk to the water's edge, trudge through the mud, kiss your baby on the face, and let the river carry him to his next appointed place. This needs to happen when the time is right, and it is rarely easy. It takes courage and grace, but it is necessary. Otherwise, all the hiding and all the protecting and all the wise strategies you have employed as a mother will fail to accomplish their ultimate purpose.

Let me encourage you to love your children enough to let go. You may want to protest at this thought. You may even want to accuse me of not understanding since I am not a mother. But let me tell you that a father must let go as well — and sometimes I think it's harder on us! Seriously, though, we parents must release our children. It is not that we turn them loose on the world or that we kick them out of our lives, it is that we realize that they must have experiences beyond our own backyards in order to fully develop their potential. They must eat from other tables and drink from other wells if they are going to be people of depth and versatility. God did not design a family to give all of its members everything they need for every experience in their lives. Love allows each one to explore, to learn, and to excel in a variety of venues, with all kinds of people.

Just consider the alternative to letting your children go: You would still be wiping chocolate off their faces when they were fifty! Just think of what a shame it would be for a forty-year-old to still live at home with his mother and play in a sandbox all day if he were destined to be the president of the

United States or the researcher who renders Alzheimer's a disease of the past!

I know the road can be rocky at first. Many a mother has made the tough but necessary decision to let her children go, only to discover that they made foolish choices or bad friends. This is the risk a mother must take. She must shift from shielding them with her hands to surrounding them with the protection of her prayers. She must allow her sons and daughters to travel from mother's loving arms to God's watchful care. And then she must trust Him.

One of the wonderful twists in Jochebed's story is that she got her baby back. Exodus, chapter two, tells us that Moses' older sister "stood afar off" watching his little basket float down the river. When she saw that Pharaoh's daughter had picked him up, she ran to the princess and asked, "Shall I go and call a nurse for you from among the Hebrew women, that she may nurse the child for you?" (Exodus 2:7). When the princess responded affirmatively, Moses' sister ran and called her mother to nurse him. God returned the child that Jochebed had released and entrusted to Him!

To every mother who thinks her children have strayed and are never to return, be encouraged. If you are mourning the loss of a personal prodigal, remember that your son or daughter will eventually long to come home. I believe that God will also restore the children you thought you lost. Good-bye does not mean they are gone forever. You keep praying. No matter how long and how hard you have prayed, keep it up. God is able to bring them back. I want you to remember that.

As we conclude this lesson, I urge you to look for the greatness in your children, remembering always that greatness takes many different forms. Whether your children are two or twenty-two or fifty-two, begin to speak to the potential that is inside of them. Nourish their dreams. Help them develop their natural gifts. Teach them how to be wise as they mature in their strengths. Keep them hidden in your house, under your nurturing wing, until the time comes for them to begin to face the world. As they take their places upon the stage of life, savor the moments, knowing that it was worth everything.

Homework for the heart: Describe a time when your mother "hid you in the house" as a child. How did you feel about such containment at the time? How do you feel now, looking back on it? What are some ways you need to hide your own children in your house? What are some ways you need to let them go?

A mother's secret prayer: Dear God, I ask that You help me to know how long to keep my children in the yard, how long to keep them hidden in my house. And, perhaps more important, let me know when to let them go and be released into the calling of their own greatness. Give me courage and strength, Lord, that I might never give up on them, but know that You are at work in their lives, bringing into fruition the seeds that I was blessed to nurture. Amen.

LESSON NINE

MAMAS TEACH US THE VALUE OF SUPPORT

Being raised in a house with a father who was infirm and unable to do so many things meant that Mom and I carried the sofa into the house. It meant that we moved the china cabinet and hauled the firewood in the snow. I tell you, I was a little boy but I had to get with the program and learn to carry loads that seemed too big for me. But when I was faced with something I could not do alone, my mother was always there to help.

To this day, I am still learning how to carry loads that I feel ill-suited to bear. I regularly find myself faced with tasks far bigger than I am, whether it is putting on our annual MegaFest conference (which is a megajob!) or walking through Louisiana in the wake of Hurricane Katrina, seeing the most enormous display of human need I have ever laid eyes on, and racking my brain to figure out what I could do to help. In daunting situations such as these, I thank

God that I can cast my cares on Him because He cares for me.

He cares for you too. In His caring, He does not just reach down from heaven and lift every burden from us. If He did, we would never mature or be strengthened. I understand the need to allow people to carry burdens they think are too heavy. As a pastor, I have had to learn to support people *through* their tough times, not to try to erase the challenges and obstacles from their lives. I cannot do the work for the parishioner — whether it is the work of forgiveness, the work of enduring suffering until a brighter day dawns, or the work of picking up pieces after a relationship has been shattered. No, my job is to provide spiritual and emotional support to people who are in times of testing and trial. Over the years, I have had to resist the temptation to do the heavy lifting for people. My compassion makes me want to lighten their loads, but that would not help them. It might provide a temporary reprieve from their burdens, but it would leave them incapacitated and weak, dependent and depleted. It would leave their mental, spiritual, and emotional muscles without the strength they need to develop.

The idea in pastoring is to show them which posture to use as they pick up the loads they must carry, to support them through their battles, not fight their battles for them. It is to help them understand how to balance the burden so that it will not knock them off their feet. It is to remind them to rest along the way, so that they can stay strong for the duration. As they walk through their hard times, my job is to cheer them on, to pat them on the back, to offer loving correction when needed, and then to celebrate with them when the journey is complete.

Maybe I learned how to support people because I had a mother who supported me. During her lifetime, I never knew what a tremendous support she was as a mother to me. It was not until her pew was empty and her phone was off that I began to feel the absence of the support I had known all of my life. I had always known she was always there — quietly, in the shadows of the spotlight that was often on me. But I never knew how her sheer presence gave me courage until it was missing. That is the thing about supporting people, and I really want you to understand this because it will help you support those who love and need you. It is not how loudly you speak or what you say, support is just being there in the corner, standing quietly, giving a nod of encouragement in moments that matter.

No one walks into a house and says, "My goodness, Mrs. Johnson, you certainly have beautiful floor joists," or "Good heavens, this house is well insulated!" Items like floor joists and insulation are silent strengths that make a house stronger and more comfortable. They are rarely seen or thought about; people do not even realize that they are part of the house, but everyone would know it if they were not.

You may be spending much of your time and energy supporting people who do not acknowledge or appreciate the great gift you are giving them. It's okay; you are like a floor joist — strong, stable, and essential, but not very obvious. Do not be sad if your value as a supporter is not recognized. Most people simply do not realize how valuable it is, especially if you have always been there. Someday, your support will be not only recognized but greatly missed.

Let me encourage you to look at ways you currently provide support to people and how you might improve. I know that you are someone's silent strength and that you can make a difference in that person's life by simply being there. Being there is enough, but being there and offering a few encouraging words, a pat on the back, or a twinkle in your eye that says, "I knew you could do it" is even better.

Everybody needs a cheerleader. Oh, I have known a few people of uncommon resolve who have made it on their own, but most people who achieve a measure of success in life have had someone who stood with them and supported them. Most likely, the soaring soprano of operatic fame had someone to say, "Come on. Stretch a little farther. You can hit that high note." The scientist on the cutting edge of research that may someday cure the illnesses that rob us of the ones we love had someone who gave him a toy microscope for Christmas when he was very young. The lean, mean athletic machine who can hit the three-pointer every time had someone who said, "Just keep practicing. Practice makes perfect."

No doubt there are budding athletes, singers, dancers, doctors, preachers, firefighters, civic leaders, pilots, and homemakers in your life, maybe even under your roof. I believe you may be surrounded with heroes who simply need some support in order to fulfill their destinies.

Take the time to go to the ball game, to attend the play, to oversee practice sessions at home. Invest in the best coaching and training opportunities available to those who need to know that you are interested in them and on their side. Ask people what they dream of doing, what they would love to do, what they long to accomplish. Engage them in conversations on those topics, and sprinkle words of affirmation and encouragement throughout the discussion.

Children and teenagers desperately need the support of an adult who is willing to invest in potential greatness, but they are not the only ones who need support. We all need it as we go through the various ages and stages of our lives. The newlyweds, the first-time parents, the young man or woman embarking on a professional journey, the middle-aged singles who do not feel they "fit" in a married world, the ill and the displaced, the man in midlife crisis, the mother whose nest is finally empty, the retired people who lose their sense of purpose when they no longer report to work, the widows and widowers — all of these people need support. They need to be loved and affirmed and given grace when they do not do everything exactly right. Every transition in life can be unnerving. Age and experience do not necessarily make the changes easier to embrace, but having someone there to support you through them does.

Not long before my mother died, I celebrated a birthday. I was scheduled to make a television appearance that evening. I wanted my mother to be there, but knew that she probably would not be able to come. She slept all day so that she would have the energy to attend my celebration at the television studio and wish me a happy birthday on TV. Now *that* is support.

Everything my mother started, she got to finish through me. Every time I have walked out onto a stage, she has shared — and she still does. That, of course, is a great blessing to me.

And so, the lesson I would pass along to you about the value of support is: appreciate the people who support you; do not let them be invisible. Though they are probably mature enough to be willing to strengthen you silently, take time to let them know how much their support means to you. Realize what a gift they are and take time to say "thank you." And then, in every possible way, every chance you get, make an effort to support someone else.

Homework for the heart: Recall a time when your mother supported and encouraged you when you were a child. Now think of a time when she has cheered you up or been uplifting for you as an adult. What do the two experiences have in common? How have you learned to support others based on what you've experienced?

A mother's secret prayer: Lord, You are my comforter, a very real help in times of trouble. Thank You for the many ways You encourage and support me, especially through the many people who cheer me on and lift me up. I pray that I may elevate my children and those I love with the same support, that they may know their gifts and exercise them for greatnesss. Amen.

SUBSTITUTE TEACHER
LEARNING FROM MAUD POWELL

It was a bright, crisp fall morning in Washington, D.C. All around me was the undercurrent that comes only from busy people who know that today is Friday and tomorrow is the blessed and sacred weekend, long awaited and deeply appreciated by working people. I moved briskly from security checkpoint to security checkpoint, armed with my son, my tape recorder, and my all-weather trench coat. I was in Washington on my way to meet with a five-star general who had surprisingly allowed me to reach him with very little preplanning. It was virtually impossible not to be awed by the idea of meeting with this man, who had taken the nation by storm.

My oldest son was walking briskly beside me, and I tried to hide the pride that I had as a father. Proud of my son, proud of my country, and proud that we were going to see an African American who was so revered

174

and so respected in a nation where my ancestors were once slaves. *I'll bet if the old slave workers who helped to build the capital could see us, they would be shocked,* I thought.

My son and I continued walking toward the office of a man who was so influential that many in the nation kept asking him to run for president of the United States — and he continually, and perhaps wisely, declined. That's right, I was going to see the then secretary of state, Mr. Colin Powell. Mr. Powell, whose leadership had been a beacon that shed light and beamed promise through the troubled times we were facing, and had withstood all of the political land mines associated with such positions, was just down the hall.

Proudly, I walked through one clearance after another, emptying out my pockets, being scanned by magnetometers multiple times, and feeling a slight bit guilty that I would dare to take up a busy man's time with a question about his mother when I knew that the leaders of the world wanted an audience with him about dangerous global affairs, toxic international conditions, and troubling domestic issues here in our own country. Still, I was proud that he had allowed me to spend a moment reminiscing about his life, his childhood, and perhaps studying the roots of what makes great men great! I wondered what type of woman had poured her soul into making him strong enough that, even when she was gone, he would still stand, erect and proud, fastened to the principles she so carefully placed within his soul.

After a brief wait on the seventh floor of an area decorated with memorabilia and several mementos of national, patriotic, and historical significance, I passed through a corridor laden with aged portraits of historic leaders. Soon we were escorted into a room filled with chandeliers and draped windows, tapestry-clad floors, and ornate antique furniture. But all decorum receded as Mr. Powell, whose presence had no competition, greeted me with the warmth of a long-lost relative who had not been seen in years. My son and I sat with him and listened as he shared with us the personal memories that traced the path leading him where he was that day. All I had to do was start the conversation and then catch the honey as it leaked from his lips, smiling occasionally. Glancing into the distant window of his past and then returning to the meeting in the room, he told us about ancestors who made their way across chilling waters, leaving

Jamaica on fruit boats to land wearily on the shore of America, where they experienced their first taste of land of the free and the home of the brave.

His mother and father were the kind of people who did not allow where they started to determine where they ended and, at the risk of life-threatening peril, made it safely to the shores of this country to give their descendants the hope of a better life. He said that his mother would often remind him, when he was tempted to be slothful or to deviate from the path of success that they had charted for him and his three siblings, "We didn't come across on the boat to raise a bum!"

As he shared these words of matriarchal wisdom with me, I could almost hear her Jamaican accent bouncing against the national archives and through the hallways of this museum of history and colorful canvas. Undoubtedly, her strong reprimand was all it took to remind the then little boy of his responsibility and the unfathomable price she and his father had paid to implement an opportunity for him. I could not help but wonder whether she had any idea that she was raising a giant, a superhero and a national diplomat whose fierce career and valiant service would reach so far beyond the impoverished, meager beginnings of rural Jamaica.

As we visited that day, it was clear that the dark, chilly waters of the Atlantic could not put out the light from the torch his mother had lit in his soul. I could still see the embers of passion burn in his middle-aged eyes as he sat and talked with me, displaying a warmth that few get to see, given that his normal public demeanor is often the more staid, stoic posture of a great American military leader.

He is a great American indeed, but he is also a grateful son, and I am honored that he would take the time and energy to allow you and me to peer through the window of his past and catch a vibrant glimpse of his extraordinary mother, who raised an extraordinary man.

MY MOTHER, MAUD ARIEL McKOY POWELL
Colin Powell

"My son, the general!" Those words passed my mother's lips with pride more times than I can count. I well remember seeing my mother as she watched me during the ceremony that crowned my rise through the ranks of the United States Army. Her Jamaican face grinning from ear to ear; her mama's heart bursting with pride; every inch of her short, round frame radiating delight; and her soul more than satisfied with my accomplishments. I suspect, though, that she was also greatly relieved that day because, in my early years, I had given her more than one reason to doubt that she would ever be able to call me successful.

You see, my success was her success. My achievements were her achievements. And for me to make it in America, well, that meant that she had made it in America too. She was born and raised amid the balmy breezes and laid-back culture of Jamaica. She was the oldest of nine children, and she ended up in the United States after her mother had immigrated here to find work. My grandmother, whom we called Gram, separated from her husband while some of her children were still young enough to be fully dependent on her. Determined to provide for them, she left Jamaica to work in Panama, then in Cuba, and eventually in America. After she was settled, she sent for my mother, who willingly left the palm trees and fresh air of the islands for the bricks and mortar of New York City, and arrived at Ellis Island to assist Gram in her work and to help provide for the younger children.

In addition to her work as a maid and as a pieceworker in the garment district, Gram also made a little money by providing room and board for some of our Jamaican relatives and other immigrants. That's where my father showed up. Luther Powell started his American journey in Philadelphia after arriving on a fruit boat from Jamaica. He then moved to New York and stayed for a time at Gram's boardinghouse in Harlem. There, he met my mother. They then fell in love, married, had my sister and me, and did everything they could to raise us well.

My sister and I were both born in Harlem, but our family moved to the South Bronx when I was six years old. My parents both worked in the garment industry — Daddy as a shipping clerk and my mother as one of the women who sewed little tags or labels in pieces of clothing. Although my mother worked full-time, I was never without a motherly influence in my life because the neighborhood was filled with "aunts." Some of these ladies were blood relatives, "real" aunts, and others were aunts by virtue of their close friendship with my mother.

I don't know exactly how to explain the significance of aunts in my upbringing except to say that all of these women lived by the same standards and their moral compasses all pointed in the same direction. They all knew what was expected of one another's children, because it was no different from what they expected of their own. In this "tribe," this group to which my family belonged, we all lived by the same code. What that means in simplest terms is that I could not get away with anything! I wasn't born a general or a soldier; I didn't possess the discipline or decorum as a boy that I now practice as a man. If I had, my aunts would not have had as much to talk about, and they would not have had to keep such a keen eye out for me in the neighborhood!

From our third-floor apartment, I had to walk five blocks to school, and I had at least one aunt on every block. All along my route to school I could look up and see an aunt hanging out her window, watching me, making sure I was doing exactly what I was supposed to be doing. If I didn't behave, then the whole network of people would know about my mischief in record time!

Yes, I guess a mother's instinct (and an aunt's, of course) was to see children behave, but my mother and my aunts were after something greater than that. They were after dignity, they were after quality, they were after success. The message from my parents and from the adults in our loose extended group was the same: "We did not leave our homeland and ride boats across the ocean to mess up our lives in America. We did not come here to fail." And because children were a reflection of the family, no one was allowed to fail.

Success and failure were not determined solely by a person's educational achievements or professional position. Our definition of success was more basic than that, and if I had to boil it down to four tenets of success, they would be these: grow up to provide for your family, contribute to society, do something worthy, never shame the family.

The first time I can remember shaming the family in a significant way took place when I was a teenager and got kicked out of church camp for drinking beer. This was especially embarrassing for my parents because they were both known as pillars in our church, St. Margaret's Episcopal. My father was the senior warden, my mother was in charge of the altar guild, my sister played the piano for the children, and I was an acolyte. We were visible and active in the church and we were good, God-fearing, religious people. I was not a disrespectful or rebellious young man, and I didn't intend to offend the church or church people with my beer drinking. Nevertheless, the escapade positively horrified my mother, and she heard about it, of course, before I arrived home. She didn't lay a hand on me, but she didn't have to. She had a *look.* I saw the look as though her face were ten feet tall and I felt as though I were standing in front of the judgment seat of God Himself. She did have some choice words for me that day, but they really were not necessary. The look said it all. I got the message: I had disgraced the family, I had brought shame upon our clan, I had made us the center of neighborhood gossip, I had woefully embarrassed my mother.

Despite that incident, I was basically a good guy. My mother didn't have cause to worry about my straying off the path of decency, but she was concerned about the lack of drive and direction that was evident in my life. I was not exactly the best student in school — not for lack of smarts, but because nothing really captured my attention. I had plenty of inborn intelligence, I just was not disciplined enough to use it. I went to college because I thought I was supposed to, not because I wanted to. During my first year at City College of New York, I finally found something I liked very much and turned out to be good at — the army. The college's ROTC (Reserve Officers' Training Corps) appealed to me and I discovered as part of that group that I had what it took not only to serve well as a soldier, but also to lead. When my mother questioned my ROTC involvement, all I could say to her was, "But Ma, I like it. And I'm good at it." It was the first time I had ever been able to talk about something that way — and the first time I had ever been able to embrace the discipline I needed.

My mother was glad to know I had found a place to excel during my studies while I prepared for a career in something besides the military (at least that's what she thought). Actually, she wanted me to go into engineering as some of my cousins had because "that was where the money was." I tried, but soon realized I was not cut out to be an engineer! I then decided to pursue a degree in geology, which I enjoyed — but not as much as the ROTC. I truly believe that everyone can find a way up in life, and the ROTC just happened to be mine.

Upon college graduation, I was infinitely

more excited about my ROTC commission than I was about my geology degree. My mother understood that I had a commitment to fulfill to the army, but continued to ask, basically, when I was going to get a real job. It wasn't until I told her that I would have a pension from the army that she began to look upon my military service as perhaps a positive endeavor after all — at least until I went to Vietnam.

After Vietnam, my mother began asking about my future plans again, saying things like: "Okay, now you've done your job. When are you getting out?" No one in our family had ever made a career in the military, and now that I had served in combat, most of the family, including my mother, thought it was time for me to move on. I had to follow my heart, though, and the longer I stayed in the army and the higher I rose through its ranks, the better my mother could accept my serving my country in that way. By the time she took her place at the ceremony in which I was promoted to general, she thought it was a great idea!

My mother has been gone for more than twenty years, but I can still see her in my mind's eye. I can still hear her voice, especially when she uttered an old Jamaican expression, a vigorous "Chuh!" which meant, "Boy, get out of here!" or "You're kidding me!" or whatever else it needed to mean at any given moment.

Other than that one-word exclamation, I don't remember any particular phrases she used often, I don't remember any family conferences, I don't remember any specific lectures she gave me. What I remember most is that a way of life — a way of living — was instilled in my sister and me through our parents. My mother didn't sit me down and counsel me, nor did she really punish me; she simply lived with the standards that were inbred in her and as I watched her, I knew what I was supposed to do. She was my standard; I could look at her and determine what was right and what was wrong, what was good and what was bad, what was noble, what was acceptable, what was questionable. She was not constantly talking "at" me, but her life spoke clearly.

The same was true for my aunts. Neither my cousins nor I could tell you exactly how we knew what we were supposed to do; we just knew, so we just did it.

My heart breaks when I realize that young people today do not have the example of mothers and fathers, grandparents, aunts (whether they are blood relatives or not!), and uncles that I had growing up. I am extremely concerned about the disintegration of the family in our modern society, and I am grieved to see that, in many areas, we are not raising children anymore. We are feeding them fast food and allowing them to be babysat by televisions — instead of wrapping our arms around them, instead of reading to them, instead of passing down the truths that we know contribute to success. As a culture, we are not giving young people the experiences they need in order to be adults; we are not transmitting the value systems and the standards of a good life. I suppose the state of the next generation in America and around the world troubles me so because I was raised so differently and I know how priceless family is. how important standards are, and how necessary proper childhood training is to effective adulthood. I suppose I learned those things from my mother.

If my mother were here today, she would not only be talking about her son the general, but also about her son the former secretary of state. Like most mothers, she would not only be bragging on me, she would also be concerned about the challenges, the responsibilities, and the controversies that accompany the lives of public servants. She would also be talking now about her son the retired general, who is doing everything he can to improve the lives of children. There's a part of her heart in me, that piece of her that longed to see people become better than their circumstances seemingly allow, that passion for people to succeed. That's what her dream was when she left Jamaica all those years ago — and, through me, that dream lives on for children everywhere.

LESSON TEN

MAMAS TEACH US TO
LOVE OURSELVES

Throughout the course of my life and ministry, particularly with my Woman, Thou Art Loosed! conferences, I often encounter women wounded by their pasts, crippled by the pain of abuse or betrayal. Many of them aren't even sure why they feel as embittered as they feel. As I've mentioned before in these pages, I feel compelled to minister to these women because of the love and support I received from my mother, because of my own hurts and brokenness and the ways that God has loved me through my parents and others throughout my life.

Sometimes, however, learning to love ourselves seems impossible. Stop for a moment and ask yourself: When was the last time you felt unloved or worthless for no apparent reason? Do you ever feel that you simply do not belong? Have you secretly felt like a misfit all of your life and never really known why? I think most of us have in one way or another, at some season of our lives along the way. Like believing in ourselves, loving ourselves can be a daunting lesson to learn, a lifelong process of growing into accepting and embracing all of who we are and were meant to be.

Numerous obstacles to our growth throw themselves in front of us like storm-tossed tree trunks blocking a roadway. Perhaps one of the largest trunks, if you will, stems from what I call a "Leah complex," the powerful impact of rejection reverberating within your soul. Let's revisit the story of Leah and her sister and the devastating experience that continues, metaphorically, to create a major stumbling block to our ability to love ourselves.

You remember the story. Two sisters, Leah and Rachel, were the daughters of a man named Laban, who was a bit of a scoundrel. One day, Jacob, the son of Isaac and the grandson of Abraham, traveled to the city of Haran, where Laban lived. Laban was his uncle, though it appears the two men had never met. When Jacob stopped to draw water from a well near Haran, he saw Rachel for the first time, and apparently she took his breath away. He ended up at Laban's house and offered to work for Laban for seven years in exchange for the privilege of marrying Rachel.

I can only imagine how excited Jacob must have been when his wedding day finally dawned. He had labored *seven years* for his bride, but the Bible says that "they seemed only a few days to him because of the love he had for her" (Genesis 29:20). She was a rich reward indeed, and I am sure that Jacob felt she was well worth every long, backbreaking day he had worked for her. Amazing, isn't it, in this time when it is hard to find a young man who appreciates the importance of a job? This young man Jacob worked like a mule, like a pack horse, for love. His amazing stamina was fueled by the intoxicating feeling he had upon every remembrance of his beloved Rachel.

In those days, a bride was heavily veiled for her wedding. There was, of course, no electricity indoors, so a man and his new wife were completely in the dark on their wedding night. Perhaps it was her veiling or perhaps it was his inability to see her beyond a sexual object. Whatever it was, he had spent the night with a woman he did not know. How many of you have been handled by a man who did not see who you really were? Jacob spent the entire night with her and never saw her face, the light in her eyes, her fears, her needs. Her voice never told him; there was no communication to help him recognize her. She was invisible in a way that no woman wants to be invisible.

The next morning, Jacob awoke to find Leah lying next to him, and needless to say, he was furious. I can see him now, throwing back the blankets on the bed and stomping off to find Laban. When he did, he demanded, "What is this you have done to me? Was it not for Rachel that I served you? Why then have you deceived me?" (Genesis 29:25).

In response, that rascal Laban replied, "It must not be done so in our country, to give the younger before the firstborn" (Genesis 29:26). Laban then proceeded to tell Jacob that he could marry Rachel if he would work an additional seven years for her, and Jacob, of course, agreed.

For years, Christians have wanted to say, "No fair!" when they read about what happened to Jacob. After all, seven years is a long time, and Laban did execute a mean and dirty scheme against him. But before we bemoan the injustice that Jacob suffered, let us remember his own past and the fact that, in league with his mother, he deceived his sick, blind, elderly father and stole his brother's birthright. He cheated his brother out of the better portion of his inheritance, so when Jacob wanted "the better portion" in the form of Rachel, he got cheated into taking someone he considered much less desirable. Hmm — sound familiar, Jacob? I have read somewhere along my journey — yes, in Galatians — that we reap what we sow. Jacob sowed deception and he reaped deception. It's that simple.

I think the true injustice in this story has to do with Leah rather than with Jacob. How must she have felt the morning after her wedding, knowing that she had been used as a trick? What must her heart have suffered when she realized that the sweet words Jacob had whispered to her and the passion he had expressed the previous evening had been intended for someone else? What must she have thought about herself as she saw Jacob's disgust when he realized he had been in bed with her all night? Only Leah could truly answer these questions, but anyone who has ever known the sting of rejection can well imagine how worthless, how utterly ashamed and totally degraded, she felt. Her self-image probably was not good to begin with, but no doubt it suffered a death blow in that moment.

We know nothing about Leah as a child or a teenager. The Bible simply provides us with this information: "Leah's eyes were delicate, but Rachel was beautiful of form and appearance" (Genesis 29:17). In other words, Rachel was more than just a pretty face — she had quite a figure too! On the other hand, Leah's eyes were not delicate in the sense of being dainty and beautiful; they were delicate in the sense of being weak, not strong; they were "dull," the Amplified Bible says. We can usually tell what is in a woman's heart by looking in her eyes. When her eyes sparkle and dance, she is a happy lady. When her eyes look like there is a bonfire blazing within them, she tends to be a passionate and determined person. When a woman's eyes are weak, her soul is usually low on strength as well.

There is a good chance that Leah had felt inferior to Rachel since her little sister was born. Leah probably grew up feeling rejected and devalued, listening to people talk about Rachel's exquisite beauty for as long as she could remember. Oh, you know the kind of conversations I am referring to. A family shows up at a church or school function or a social event. Someone walks up and says to one child: "Oh, aren't you a beautiful little girl?" and to the other, "and I'll bet you are very sweet." Or, perhaps it goes like this: "Have you met the Jones family yet? They are the ones with the tall, slender daughter who is so pretty — and then they have another daughter too."

Yes, Leah was always "the other daughter" and she knew it — "other daughters" always do. Her father knew it too, and though we can give him the benefit of the doubt and say that he sent her to Jacob as a way of ensuring marriage for her, I believe that his actions sealed her low self-esteem for the rest of her life. His job as a father in those days was to arrange the best possible marriage for his daughters, but instead, he arranged the worst for Leah. Why? Because he knew that Jacob's heart belonged to Rachel; he knew that Jacob's affections would never turn toward Leah. In making her marry Jacob, he forever took away any opportunity for her to be loved. Perhaps there was a young man in Haran who would have found her attractive. Perhaps someone would have wanted her. Perhaps someone would have fallen in love with her, if only Laban had given her a chance.

Leah's marriage to Jacob must have been unbearable for her. There she was, knowing that he awakened every morning with the thought that he was one day closer to marrying Rachel and that he went to bed at night sick with desire for her. By the time

Jacob did finally marry Rachel, Leah had been with him for seven long years. Perhaps she hoped he would get over Rachel. Maybe she spent those years wearing herself out trying to be such a good wife that he would decide to do without Rachel after all. In the pit of her heart, though, she knew better. The voice of rejection played over and over in her mind, reminding her that she was not her husband's first choice.

Nevertheless, she was Jacob's wife and they lived together as married people do. Leah became pregnant and began to bear sons. When her first child, Reuben, was born, she said, "The Lord has surely looked on my affliction. Now therefore, my husband will love me" (Genesis 29:32). When her second son, Simeon, came along, she said, "Because the Lord has heard that I am unloved, He has therefore given me this son also" (Genesis 29:33). When her third son was born, she named him Levi, believing, "This time my husband will become attached to me, because I have borne him three sons" (Genesis 29:34). No joy accompanied the birth of these boys. With comments such as Leah's, we cannot believe that she was an excited new mother; we can only have compassion for this tragic, wretched figure — this desperate, desperate woman.

I want to pause here and write for a moment to every woman who has ever felt the need to earn her husband's love, to every woman who has ever felt that, even when his body was in bed with her, his heart was somewhere else. Let me ask you to look deep within your heart and examine the motives behind your actions toward your man. Have you felt unloved and tried to evoke his affections with certain behaviors? Have you been trying to do things — to "perform" — in order to be loved or even to feel loved (and there is a difference) or attempted to solicit compliments, comments, or positive feedback because you simply need to hear him voice his approval of you? If you, like Leah, have labored in vain to produce results you thought would surely cause him to love you, then it is time to take a rest. It is time to stop straining, striving, and trying to earn what can only be given.

I need to tell you that you cannot force a man to love you. Leah could not do it with three fine sons, and you cannot do it with anything you could dream up. You can, however, drive him farther away with your desperation. Attempting to get a man to do or say things that are not in his heart to do or say, especially to meet your own emotional need, is called manipulation. Women who struggle with rejection tend to be quite skilled at this controlling type of talk and behavior. They have had years of practice, because they have a history of needing affirmation and have learned how to get it. But manipulation leads to trouble. Many times, a woman who struggles with rejection attracts a man who wrestles with it too. Instead of finding true acceptance in each other, they end up pushing each other farther and farther away. Oh, they may soar on the gusts of passion for a while, but when the winds die down and real life demands to be lived, they find that passion did not heal their feelings of rejection, it only did a good job of covering them up. At other times, a rejected woman will attract a man who is passive and peace-loving. He will cooperate with her manipulation, simply because he does not want to confront it. That does not heal her rejection, either; it only perpetuates it.

Whether you are married or single, if you are longing to be loved (and my single sisters, do not be deceived; there are married women who still long for love — just like Leah) and have suffered the pain of rejection, stop looking for another human being to fill the void in your heart. Your desire can only be satisfied in God. You need to know right now that no man's love will ever be enough for you — and it is not supposed to be. There is only one who can hear the silent cries of your heart and meet your deepest needs. His name is Jesus. Whatever you have done or not done, He loves you just the same. Whether you succeed brilliantly or fail miserably, He loves you just the same. When everything is going your way, and when everything seems to go south, He loves you just the same. His love is not dependent upon your behavior. You cannot earn His acceptance. In fact, He is completely unimpressed with any effort to do so and graciously brushes off such attempts. He understands that the only reason we try to perform for Him is that we do not know any better; we have not yet received the revelation that He accepts us just exactly the way we are.

"What about my sin?" you ask. "How could He love me after the things I've done?" Oh, I have had women cry and say to me countless times in counseling sessions, "But, Bishop, you don't know what I have done! You don't know how awful I have been!" Hear me: I do not need to know what *you* have done, because I know what *Jesus* has done. And what Jesus Christ did on the cross at Calvary trumps anything you could ever do on earth. He is much more aware of the power of the blood than we are. He takes you seriously when you ask His forgiveness; He wipes your slate clean. If you are a believer in Jesus Christ, God sees you as righteous, radiant, and pure. You make His heart sing. You are totally accepted and extravagantly loved.

A woman who has found her place in the love of God is a strong, secure, confident woman indeed. She is able to love and accept herself and she walks through life with a wholeness that begins in her soul and spreads to every aspect of her being. She needs nothing from anyone, because she has found everything in God. This kind of woman puts no demands on her husband. Because she knows God's love and acceptance, she does not try to pull out of her husband what he does not have to offer. She knows that he is not God, so she goes to God to get what only He can give. She knows that God has designed marriage in such a way that she will have needs her husband can and should meet, but she relieves him of any expectation to provide her with her sense of worth and value. She does not demand his love as her right or his duty; she receives it as his gift and it becomes her treasure.

My prayer is that the man you have deemed worthy enough to give your love to will love you back, that he will be every good thing God has ordained him to be for you, that his love for you will be strong and deep, tender and passionate and true. But more than that, I pray that you will know and experience the settled satisfaction of God's unconditional love for you, the richness of the Lord's unquenchable passion for you, the joy of knowing His unceasing delight in you — and that you will love yourself as He loves you. As you do, all of your relationships, including your marriage, will be set free to reach their greatest potential, fulfill their highest purpose, and bring maximum enjoyment to you and those you love.

If you have ever struggled as Leah did, I believe that your life will take a turn for the better as you keep reading her story and learning from her. You see, something happened to her between the time Levi was born and the birth of her next child. In that interval, a shift occurred in her heart. We do not know what happened or how it transpired, but we see its results when her fourth son is born: "Now I will praise the Lord," she said — and she called the boy Judah, which means "praised." By this time, Leah had made peace with herself and her situation, perhaps with Jacob too. She had accepted the realities of her life, even though she would have preferred them to be different. She had reached the place where she had to choose whether to keep living with the unfulfilled longings that made her miserable or whether to release all her disappointments, her past rejection, and her feelings of worthlessness to the Lord. She chose the release — and that enabled her to praise.

When a woman releases her pain to God, He moves in like a soft shower of healing rain and gives her a long, gentle soak. Letting go of the hurt is not always easy. Releasing rejection has its challenges. Sometimes a woman's pain or difficulty provides her with her identity. She may not necessarily like being called "the one whose husband left her for his secretary" or "the one with all the health problems" or "the one whose son robbed the convenience store" or "the one who got laid off," but strangely, she realizes that those descriptions do apply. Especially if she has been referred to in certain ways over a long period of time, she begins to believe them and starts to act in ways that reinforce them.

The thought of letting God heal her can be daunting because she has been known by her circumstances for so long that she wonders who she will be and what she will do if He does. Surrendering the wounds of your heart to the God who heals does require courage, but I promise you that it is a risk worth taking. He is a wise and compassionate God, skillfully mending your soul and putting your broken heart back together again. He will touch your tender places ever so gently; He will heal you in the deepest ways and restore you completely. All you have to do is ask — and let Him have your pain.

When God begins to heal your heart, you cannot help but praise Him. With healing comes wholeness, strength, boldness, new vision for your life, a fresh burst of energy, joy, confidence, and the ability to minister to others. The healing of the Lord eliminates your craving for love and affirmation from other people and enables you to value yourself because He values you. It will enable you to stop giving birth to the Reubens, the Simeons, and the Levis in your life and to bring forth in their place a steady stream of praise.

Even though Leah learned to praise, her struggles were not over. She had to deal with the fact that Rachel was barren and exceedingly envious of her fertility. We are going to look at jealousy in the next chapter, but for now, I simply want to encourage you to remember how much God loves you and how thoroughly He accepts you. As a way of honoring Him, learn to love yourself too. A woman who loves herself in a godly way makes for a strong mother and teaches her children by example how to value themselves too.

I also urge you to combat rejection in your children. Make sure you tell them often how much you love them and how much God loves them. Let them know that you may not approve of everything they *do* (and that you will have to enforce discipline at those times), but that you absolutely adore who they *are.*

Bless your children every chance you get. Do everything you can to make sure they grow up feeling valued and celebrated. From the time they are very young, tell your daughters often how beautiful they are. Tell them how smart and special they are.

And for yourself, if you have felt like Leah all of your life, then it is time to break those chains of rejection that have held you down for so long and begin to feel as Rachel did — desperately wanted, treasured, worth waiting for. To Jesus, you are a woman worth dying for; He has bought you with His blood and you belong to Him. He wants you to esteem yourself very highly. Ask Him to heal your heart and to reveal how mightily He loves you. Ask Him to let you see yourself in His mirror, as He sees you. Believe that you are beautiful and desirable — because God says you are.

As the father of my two daughters, I try to make sure they realize how much they are worth. My daughter Cora's voice raises when she is happy. She can make you laugh until your sides hurt. She loves children. She will give you anything she has. Her heart is big — sometimes too big. My daughter Sarah is smart as a whip; she is domestic and sophisticated. We always tease her about the way she talks, faster and faster the more excited she becomes. I see my daughters as jewels, gifts from heaven, stars in the crown of my life. They are stunningly beautiful young women, both inside and out. That is why I tell them, "When you find a man who loves you like Daddy does, then he is the one."

Maybe you never had a father to love you like that. But guess what? You have a heavenly Father who loves you in a way that is indescribable. Do you know what marriage is meant to be? It is meant to be a chance for God to love you through the arms of one of His sons. Treat your husband like he is a gift to you and expect to be treated like you are a gift to him. Together you will find that your relationship is simply your heavenly Father living in both of you through each other's arms.

True love is a ministry given by God through His children to each other. It is a safe place for a wind-driven ship to dock and rest from the ill winds of life. True love is a deep-cleaning medicine that heals the infections of childhood and pains of adult rejections. It is worth the wait to get it right. No, you are not looking for a perfect man. There are none. What you are looking for is a perfect or mature love. A mature love can love even flaws and broken places. In order to get it, you have to give it.

And in order to get it and to give it, you have to experience it supernaturally from your Heavenly Father. In case you've forgotten, let me remind you that you are etched into the palm of God's hand, that you are continually before Him and that He loves you with an everlasting love (see Isaiah 49:16; Jeremiah 31:3). Always remember that He is rejoicing over you with gladness and singing, bringing a hush to all the noise in your life with His love (see Zephaniah 3:17). Tell yourself again and again that nothing can separate you from the love of God that is yours in Christ Jesus — "neither death nor life, nor angels nor principalities nor powers, nor things present nor things to come, nor height nor depth," as the Apostle Paul wrote in Romans 8:38, 39 — and I would add that neither your past nor your pain, nor your broken heart nor your broken home, nor what others say about you nor what you say about yourself, nor any other force in all the universe can *ever* cause God to turn His love away from you. Fling open the doors of your heart and let His love rush in; receive His acceptance and revel in His affection for you.

You are lovable and worth loving because God created you and loves you, no matter what. No matter how many Jacobs reject you or how many Rachels slight you or how many Labans trade you, you are a pure and beautiful jewel, loved by God. Treat yourself as His and you will overcome any obstacle, from the tree limbs to the trunks of redwoods, that may litter your path. You are loved!

Homework for the heart: What did your mother teach you about loving yourself? In which ways did she disappoint you and create obstacles to loving yourself? What's the greatest obstacle to loving yourself right now as you read this page? How can you accept the truth about who you are and how much God loves you and move forward?

A mother's secret prayer: Dear God, I thank You for the way You love me no matter what has happened in my past or how unlovable I may feel. I pray that I will love my own children with Your divine unconditional and never-failing love, that this will offer balm for the painful rejections of life and love affairs gone wrong. Like Leah, I ask that I choose to praise You no matter how difficult life may feel. Thank You for loving me, Lord, and for making me worth loving. Amen.

LESSON ELEVEN
MAMAS TEACH US TO
CELEBRATE OTHERS

Sisters! Lord, have mercy! We can't live with them, and we can't live without them. I have a sister, but being a man with a sister may not be as challenging as being a woman with one. Bickering and subtle rivalries plague the relationship of many female siblings. Maybe it is because we men put so much pressure on you; I don't know. But what I do know is that it starts early and often doesn't end from diapers to bedpans! Yes, I have seen this dynamic between sisters from playpens to nursing homes. I'm afraid that it's a timeless trick that the enemy uses to keep us from discovering the power of agreement.

Now you know that if natural sisters have challenges, spiritual sisters can really be challenging too. A church sister can be a beast! Believe me, I have been a pastor for a long time; I know that even when sisters are trying to do something that they agree on doing, sometimes they disagree on how it should be done and who should do what.

I once thought this discord was exclusive to church sisters, wondering if it came from something they laced the communion cups with! But this problem is just as prevalent with corporate women. They will smile at the water fountain and then destroy each other on the computer. If e-mails ever go public, there will be war in many offices!

While I confess that such backstabbing and competition are just as rampant in men at times, I find that many women repeatedly ask me for help in getting along with their sisters as envy and rivalry rock their relationships.

My mother certainly demonstrated a spirit of peace and cooperation with her own sisters and other women with whom she worked. But perhaps I've learned the most about how women, and men for that matter, can overcome jealousy by looking at that pair of famous sisters we met just a few pages ago.

In our previous chapter, we focused on Leah and how she handled rejection, but now I want to shift our gaze to Rachel because even though she was the pretty one, the desired one, she was not perfect. For there came a point at which something so ugly developed inside her that her outer beauty hardly mattered anymore. Within the woman who had been described as "beautiful of form and appearance" arose the green-eyed monster.

With so much going for her, what did Rachel have to be envious of? Even though she had to wait fourteen years, she and Jacob were finally allowed to marry, right? Yes, and I'm sure they were ecstatic. However, Rachel, like many brides, could hardly wait to give Jacob children. But she could not. The Bible specifically tells us, "When the Lord saw that Leah was unloved, He opened her womb. But *Rachel was barren*" (Genesis 29:31, italics mine).

I believe that only a barren woman can understand the desperation and the devastation of being unable to have children. Even today, in a society that seems to devalue motherhood and prioritize other things like careers and affluence, I still have women of all ages coming up to me, asking for prayer, saying, "I want to have a child." Some of them are newly married and in their twenties. Others are in their thirties and forties and are now ready for a family, but fear they may have missed their time. Proverbs 30:15–16 informs us that the barren womb is one of only four things on earth that are never satisfied. So not only did Rachel find herself in a state of frustration, anger, and grief month after month, she also saw that conceiving and bearing children seemed to be no problem at all for Leah. And there you have it: the stage was perfectly set for full-scale envy.

In fact, the stage is always set for envy or jealousy when one person has something another one wants. I once read a definition of jealousy that suggests that jealousy results when one person becomes hostile against another because of a perceived advantage. (Sometimes one person's adoration of you can make another person cynical toward you.) The advantage does not have to be a tangible thing. And once they perceive success in your life, you are a candidate for jealousy and envy, which often manifest themselves in childish but dangerous behavior.

Truly, Leah had what Rachel wanted, what Rachel was *desperate* for. Leah did not have to say a word in order to break Rachel's heart. All she had to do was rise from her seat at the sound of a baby's cry. When a deep desire is denied for too long, it gets blown all out of proportion and becomes almost a person's sole focus in life. When a deep desire is denied to one person and seems to come easily to another, especially if the two are in a close relationship, the one who wants and doesn't get it can go through a horrific kind of emotional torture called "jealousy." Whether a person is five years old or forty-five, jealousy is a destructive force in the heart of an individual and in relationships.

Jealousy starts early. We see it in toddlers when their newborn siblings come home from the hospital. Even if they cannot speak clearly, they know when someone else has commandeered the parental attention that once belonged to them and they know how to demand it back. As they grow, they have to be taught to share; otherwise they will march right up to a young friend and snatch a toy or doll right out of the other child's hands. This is the beginning of a critical life lesson: that they cannot always have everything they want exactly when they want it. If young children do not learn this lesson, a little seed of jealousy settles into the soil of their young hearts and begins to take root and to spread like a bad weed through the rest of their lives.

Now, come on, you cannot be a mother reading this book and not have noticed that little children learn this without ever taking a class on it. Half of the challenge of parenting is to avoid the perception of favoring one child over another. I have twins and I never bought something for one without buying something for the other. Even then, they would debate over who had the best color or whose car would run faster. In a young person's life, envy over toys and games soon gives way to bigger things, like bicycles or a telephone in one's room. And then, of course, in the preteen and teenage years, it involves positions on sports teams, boyfriends and girlfriends, and parts in the school play before it moves on to cars and prom dates. Young adults wrestle the green-eyed monster over admittance to certain universities, or over jobs and salaries. Throughout life, people can be envious of someone else's home, position in society, opportunities, natural gifts, or spouse.

A jealous woman is a miserable woman because she never knows the inner peace of satisfaction. She is often cranky and cross, bitter and sour. She may be incapable of deep, intimate, fulfilling relationships because she cannot support or celebrate others. Her soul churns and stews all of the time not simply because she does not have what she wants, but because someone else does. You see, jealousy does not reveal itself simply because a woman's desires go unmet. She may be empty, unfulfilled, and sick with longings, but she is not jealous. Jealousy rears its ugly head only when her sister, or her best friend, or her neighbor, or her daughter receives the very thing she so desperately wants.

Now before you start shouting and thinking about who you know that this chapter applies to, hold on a minute. Some lady who works with you may be reading this book too and thinking about you! What I am saying is that jealous people seldom have the ability to admit that they are jealous. They hide their hostility beneath the flimsy excuses they use to justify their acrimonious dispositions. They tell themselves that they have a right to dislike someone — often over the very thing that they secretly wish they had. Jealousy is stealthy and deceitful. It is cunning and can remain untraceable to those who are held in its grip. So, I have a question: Are you jealous of anyone? Could this chapter be about you?

A woman whose heart is whole does not begrudge others their good fortune. No, she refuses to allow her disappointments to become her downfall (because after all, the source of jealousy is disappointment), but she releases them to God quickly, asks Him to heal her heart, and renews her faith and trust in Him. This way, she is glad when others are glad. She shares their happiness. She rejoices when good things happen to them — even the good things that she aches for in her own life and does not have. She knows that God does not play favorites and that her time of rejoicing is on its way. She has her own life to live, her own race to run — and she knows that God will equip her with every good thing she needs along the way. She is patient and trusting, fully confident that He has heard the cries of her heart and will answer in His timing and according to His plan. She rests in the security of His love for her, knowing that He is working things out for her good and that His heart longs to bless her.

Too often women, instead of resting in the love of God and the uniqueness of their individuality, find themselves comparing and competing. Mothers (and fathers) often do this with their children, comparing everything from who was potty-trained first to who made the honor roll to who scored the winning basket. When it comes to motherhood specifically, not only do some women envy others the successes or abilities of their children, there is also a unique type of deeply painful envy known only to the women whose arms are empty and whose breasts are dry — women in whose chest a mother's heart beats, but whose wombs will not conceive. This is a condition that has broken women's hearts since ancient times. It is the profound and piercing pain that Rachel knew so well.

Let me encourage you to be sensitive to the childless couples you know. Wanting to know when a couple plans to start a family is a natural curiosity, but often an inappropriate question. With the inability to conceive and bear a child — whether through a condition in a woman or in her husband — often comes tremendous frustration, anger, despair, grief, and envy. This kind of envy may cause a woman to turn down invitations to baby showers and to stay home from church on Mother's Day. A woman forced to face infertility is not only envious, she is in great pain. Many women do not care for such an intimate situation to become public knowledge. Give her the gracious gift of privacy. Those who truly are struggling with an inability to conceive will choose the people in whom they want to confide — and those who do not will make their intentions and plans to begin or expand their family known in the timing that is right for them, so make sure that your wonderings and questions do not stoke the fire of envy that may be searing a woman's soul.

As prevalent as jealousy and envy are, there is a way to live free of them. It is possible to escape the clutches of the green-eyed monster. The vaccination is a whole heart — a heart that has received the love of God and embraced His grace, a heart that is at peace with His plans and satisfied with His provision. Once jealousy or envy has infested a person's soul, the cure for it is forgiveness. For some, this seems a bitter pill to swallow, for forgiveness is rarely easy, but it is the remedy that will keep a heart from terminal misery. As I wrote earlier, the cause of jealousy or envy is disappointment. They are but a fruit that has disappointment, broken dreams, and unmet expectations for its root system. Most of the time, disappointment leads to anger, and often to feelings of injustice as well. These emotions, when left to run their course, lead to jealousy. And so, whether you need to forgive another person, yourself, or even God for the disappointments in your life, let me urge you to do so, no matter how difficult, because that is your first step to freedom and to the joy that comes when you are at liberty to enjoy the blessings in other people's lives without resenting them.

I believe that one of the most powerful ways to defeat jealousy is to balance the books in your own heart and decide that what God has for you, is for you! Do you know that God has given you everything you need to fulfill His purpose in your life? You are a success based on His intent and what He had in mind for you when He created you. There is always someone who has something you don't. But they have it because they need it for the purpose of God in their lives. If you needed that attribute to fulfill your destiny, He would have given it to you.

Now, wait a minute. I am not saying that many things cannot be developed in you. We can exercise and enhance what God has given us; we can educate and increase what God has given us. But there are some things that training will not rectify or provide. For these things, you must come to a place of alignment where you accept the will of God and balance your heart with the sweet assurance that He is in control of your life. Disappointment can be terrible, but purpose and prayer will defeat it every time. Don't allow people to make harsh and ignorant comparisons. Who can compare with you? You are an original, a one-of-a-kind production, uniquely and fearfully made, created and designed to fulfill a destiny that is exclusively yours. There can be no contenders because you are in a category all by yourself.

Great lady, I want to remind you today of your beauty, your value, your worth. There is treasure inside of you. You need not be jealous of anyone else for any reason. You are far too noble for such pettiness. You have something to give to your sisters. You may not have the same gifts, talents, or resources that they have, but you have so much to offer them out of your uniqueness. Whether these women are part of your biological family or whether you are related only because you are traveling the same path through life, you need one another. Refuse to be jealous. Instead, encourage other women, affirm their strengths, celebrate their talents and abilities, appreciate what they can do that you cannot, let them help you in areas where you are weak. All over the earth, there is a great host of women and there is a great company of mothers. You need one another. You can accomplish so much more together than you ever could alone. In fact, you can change your world if you will link arms with others, support them and cheer them on. But in order to do so, you will have to declare war on jealousy and envy — and begin to celebrate your sisters instead.

Homework for the heart: Do you consider yourself a jealous or envious person? Why or why not? Who are you jealous of in your life right now? What does she have that you feel you do not? Learning how to overcome these feelings takes time. One of the best ways I know to overcome them is to practice gratitude for what you do have. Starting with at least three specific lessons that your mother taught you, make a list of items that you are especially grateful for this day.

A mother's secret prayer: My loving Heavenly Father, thank you for all that You so graciously give me, as well as for those things that I do not have. Please allow my heart to be contented and at peace because of who I am as Your daughter instead of being at unrest because of who I'm not when I compare myself to other women. Remove jealousy and envy from my heart and let me count the many blessings that You give me. Amen.

LESSON TWELVE
MAMAS TEACH US TO BANISH THE BITTERNESS

Of all the barriers to experiencing love, whether romantic or relational, familial or familiar, perhaps none has deeper, more insidious roots than bitterness. My mother certainly had cause to be bitter about her life, particularly after my father became ill and could no longer provide for our family and instead became another dependent. When her daughter was diagnosed with a brain tumor, my mother could easily have become bitter. But through these trials and many more, Mama weeded her garden daily of the creeping roots of bitterness that tried to penetrate the soil of her heart. She'd tell me that she didn't have time for self-pity and that her faith was in the Lord. She told me she was grateful for how He'd provided for her so far and knew that He wouldn't leave her now. My mother was no saint but she helped me to learn firsthand how important it is to overcome any seeds of bitterness that might try to implant themselves within me.

Just think for a moment of what happens when we allow ourselves to indulge this harsh harvest. You, like most of us, have probably encountered a bitter woman somewhere along your journey through life. Perhaps she took your order at a restaurant and set your plate in front of you more forcefully than necessary. Perhaps you had to step quickly out of her way as she tore down the aisle of the grocery store and grabbed a can of peas. Maybe you saw her march to her mailbox, grab her mail, and then storm back into her house as you played in your front yard. Maybe she was your second-grade teacher or your basketball coach. Maybe she was your mother; maybe she is you. All of us know someone who is as bitter and mean as a junkyard dog.

The Bible teaches us that we can tell what is inside of people because of the "fruit," the "produce," if you will, of their lives. And most of us have tasted the fruit of a bitter life — the negativity, the cynicism, the complaining and murmuring, the refusal to hope, the anger or even the rage, the huffing and puffing, the frustrated sighs. Oh yes, we know a bitter woman by her fruit.

I believe that bitterness is an extremely

dangerous condition of the soul. It is like venom flowing through the bloodstream of a person, and its potential for destruction is enormous. Like poison, it may be untraceable and only noticeable by its effect on the person who has ingested it. It is harmful to anyone who harbors it, but it is especially dangerous in a mother, for it poisons her relationships with her children and causes them to grow up to be angry, resentful, jealous, negative, and downright unpleasant too. For that reason, I would like us to look together in this chapter at the dangers of bitterness — and at the remedies.

This problem you may be dealing with as a woman or as a mother is not a new one at all. I am always amazed at how many people think they are the only one dealing with an issue. They fail to realize that issues like these are not new or exclusive to them alone. Bitterness as a problem of the human condition is as ancient as humanity itself. We read about it in several places in the Bible, but I think it is dealt with most poignantly — and most hopefully — in the short Old Testament book of Ruth because there, we see bitterness banished from a woman's life. We read about a cynical, skeptical, complaining woman who finds new strength, new hope, new purpose, and new joy in life. If such a turnaround could happen to her, it can happen to you, and to those you love as well.

In this beautiful story of romance and redemption, a woman named Naomi and her family had moved from Bethlehem to a place called Moab. While they were there, her two sons married Moabite women, but the sons soon died, as did Naomi's husband. Because of a famine in the land of Moab, Naomi decided to move back to Bethlehem. Her daughters-in-law, Ruth and Orpah, wanted to go with her, but she believed they would be better off staying in their homeland, remaining near their families and finding new husbands. Let's look at this emotional moment as Scripture records it:

And Naomi said to her two daughters-in-law, "Go, return each to her mother's house. The LORD deal kindly with you, as you have dealt with the dead and with me. The LORD grant that you may find rest, each in the house of her husband." So she kissed them, and they lifted up their voices and wept. And they said to her, "Surely we will return with you to your people." But Naomi said, "Turn back, my daughters; why will you go with me? Are there still sons in my womb, that they may be your husbands? Turn back, my daughters, go — for I am too old to have a husband. If I should say I have hope, if I should have a husband tonight and should also bear sons, would you wait for them till they were grown? Would you restrain yourselves from having husbands? No, my daughters; for it grieves me very much for your sakes that the hand of the LORD has gone out against me!" (Ruth 1:8–13)

Notice the last sentence of this passage, for it contains our first glimpse into Naomi's heart and mind. Her declaration "for the hand of the LORD has gone out against me" lets us know that she is a bitter woman. (People who blame God for their hardships always are.) Nevertheless, beneath the bitterness was a woman Ruth had grown to love. People like Naomi often shove others away and then cry when they are gone. Not everyone is as courageous or as loyal as Ruth was. Look at Orpah, who gave up and basically said to Naomi, "Okay. Have it your way." In essence, she decided that she was tired of trying to break through this woman's hard exterior. I have counseled or ministered to countless women who unconsciously make it hard for others to love them. They seem to be meanest to people who are the closest to them. People who have been hurt learn quickly how to lash out at others. They often make it hard for others to love them and then grieve because their children or husbands have decided that life is too short to live in a house with a brawling woman. The Bible says that it is better to live on the rooftop (see Proverbs 21:9). And many times, people move away rather than fight to stay connected. Orpah was that way. She said, "I am out of here!" Not Ruth. She was in for the long haul.

We can assume that Ruth had known Naomi in happier times. Perhaps Naomi had welcomed Ruth into her family with warmth and joy when Ruth married her son, or taught Ruth valuable lessons about being a wife. Maybe she had been the kind of mother-in-law that every woman would want. Whatever the reason, Ruth had a daughterly kind of affection for Naomi, and against Naomi's strongest protests, Ruth resolved to stay with Naomi when she moved back to Bethlehem. In fact, the Bible says Ruth "clung to her" — and proclaimed her loyalty to her mother-in-law with beautiful words that may be familiar to you:

Entreat me not to leave you,
Or to turn back from following after you;

For wherever you go, I will go;
And wherever you lodge, I will lodge;
Your people shall be my people,
And your God, my God.
Where you die, I will die,
And there will I be buried.
The LORD do so to me, and more also,
If anything but death parts you and me.
(Ruth 1:16–17)

After such a stirring display of commitment, Naomi stopped trying to talk Ruth into staying in Moab. Orpah did return to her family, but Ruth's face was set like flint toward Bethlehem. She wanted to be with Naomi, she wanted to live among Naomi's people, and she wanted to know and worship Naomi's God. So she turned her back on everything she had ever known — and followed a bitter old woman to Bethlehem.

Sometimes people try to hide their bitterness, or to deny it, especially when they know better. They may try to cover it up with lipstick on a smile so forced that it is painful. They may try to forget about it by spending too many hours at the office. They may try to fix it with cosmetic surgery or escape it by taking an exotic vacation. They may ignore it by pouring all of their energies into their children so that they are too tired to think about their own pain at the end of the day. Not Naomi. Take a look at what she said when she arrived back in her hometown with Ruth.

Now the two of them went until they came to Bethlehem. And it happened, when they had come to Bethlehem, that all the city was excited because of them; and the women said, "Is this Naomi?"

But she said to them, "Do not call me Naomi; call me Mara, for the Almighty has dealt very bitterly with me. I went out full, and the LORD has brought me home again empty. Why do you call me Naomi, since the LORD has testified against me, and the Almighty has afflicted me?"

So Naomi returned, and Ruth the Moabitess her daughter-in-law with her, who returned from the country of Moab. Now they came to Bethlehem at the beginning of barley harvest. (Ruth 1:19–22)

No, sir. Naomi had no trouble announcing to the entire town that she was no longer Naomi, which means "pleasantness," but Mara, which means "bitter." Isn't it something how we can change what people expect from us by broadcasting, "I am moody," "I am tired," or "I am just outspoken," or whatever we want people to expect of us. Once we go public with a hateful attitude, that kind of announcement alleviates any need to have to improve. Naomi had changed her name and thereby given herself permission to show off. This is what the Bible means when it says to not make provisions for the flesh, to fulfill its lusts (see Romans 13:14). It is easy to make provisions for the personality we have assumed. Naomi changed her name to protect herself from anyone expecting her to be joyous. What about you? Have you allowed divorce, depression, or some other problem to change your name or to change what people expect of you?

She arrived back in Bethlehem with quite an attitude. I am sure some of it could be attributed to grief, which is understandable, but she had gone overboard. Her old friends did not even recognize her. Maybe that is because bitterness can turn a person into someone she really is not. It can make a once-happy person down and depressed. It can make a once-caring person hardhearted and self-centered. It can make someone who was once pleasant bitter indeed — just like Naomi.

We know little about Naomi and her family except what we read in the four chapters of the book of Ruth. We do not know all of the circumstances under which they moved from Bethlehem to Moab or what all happened while they were there. We do know that Naomi suffered the loss of her husband and her two sons — and that is enough to make any woman bitter if she does not handle her grief appropriately. In fact, bitterness really comes from failure to handle any strong negative emotion properly. Anger, jealousy, hurt, pride, unforgiveness, even fear, can turn to bitterness if they fester too long in a person's soul.

Christians are as susceptible to bitterness as anyone else. You cannot convince me that our pain hurts any less than anyone else's or that our pride is more palatable than the next person's simply because we are believers in Jesus Christ. Do not be tempted to think that just because you have said a million times, "Oh, God, forgive me of my sins" that you could not allow bitterness to sneak into your soul. Your heartfelt prayer brings God's forgiveness, immediately and completely. But if you do not forgive yourself as fully and freely as He forgives you and if you hold on to the pain, the guilt, the anger, or the sense of injustice you have felt, then those thoughts and emotions will take root in your heart and mind and bitterness will begin to grow like an ugly, unwanted weed in a beautiful garden.

A bitter woman typically raises bitter children. Just as crack addicts have crack babies, a bitter woman has bitter sons and daughters. Her bitterness is passed down to her children through the milk of her parenting, just as any other harmful substance can be transmitted from mother to child. To be sure, children learn what they see, and inevitably they act out what their parents acted out in themselves and around the children. Recently, when I was in Kenya, where we were digging wells for water to help quench the thirst of rural indigenous people who suffered from the lack of water, a group of students did several skits for me to show me what it was like to be who they are. They did not speak my language, so they had to act out their life's story. There I was in the bush in Africa watching a Broadway production done in a simplistic but powerful way.

I was amazed at how they acted like their parents. They dressed up in their clothes and pretty soon I knew the parents by observing the behavior of the children. Similarly our children often act out what they learned from us. They may not tell others what we did, but they show them by how they themselves process issues and respond to circumstances. You and I have to admit that even though all of us have certain things we said we would never do like our parents, we still find ourselves doing it.

A bitter mother's children have no choice but to be around her, constantly exposed to and influenced by the acrimony in her soul. Because that is all they know, that is the way they grow up. The words that a bitter woman speaks to her children are like thumbtacks pressed into their tender hearts. The looks she gives them are like daggers piercing their souls. The influence she exerts over them is negative, not positive; it offers no hope to them for the future; it discourages rather then encourages them; and it causes them to see other people and the world as enemies to be mistrusted instead of friends to be enjoyed. They perceive and embrace as their own her acidic perspective on life.

Let me say once more that cynicism and bitterness are inherited. Do not let it take root in your life. Instead, keep your heart clean and tender before God and in your relationships with other people. The writer of Hebrews instructs us well in this regard: "Pursue peace with all people, and holiness, without which no one will see the Lord:

looking carefully lest anyone fall short of the grace of God; lest any root of bitterness springing up cause trouble, and by this many become defiled" (Hebrews 12:14–15).

The Bible is clear that bitterness causes trouble and defiles people. This does not have to happen. With God, a heart can be healed and a broken person can be made strong, vibrant, and joyful, a bitter woman can become a fountain of delight to everyone around her. Let's look back at Naomi's story and consider the transformation that took place in her heart.

Naomi was worn out by the time she got back home to Bethlehem. I am sure she felt that her days of being needed and being productive were behind her. After all, her husband was gone, her sons — her legacy — had died and she had no grandchildren. In her grief and despair, she had probably bought into the lie that not only did no one need her anymore, but that no one wanted her either. She was wrong! Her best days were ahead of her and she did not even know it.

Naomi's first good move was to leave the land of Moab, a place of rampant idolatry, and head back to Bethlehem. The name of the city Bethlehem means "house of bread," and it was located in the land of Judah, which symbolizes praise. When bitterness knocks on the door of your heart, get out of the places where God is not, stop worshipping the idols of self-pity or your own personal rights. Stop building monuments to your disappointments and get back to the house of bread — the place of God's nourishing presence and provision in the land of praise. Start giving God praise even when you do not feel like doing so. Press through the pain and begin to worship Him. That's the moment your situation will begin to turn around.

Naomi did struggle when she first arrived in Bethlehem, declaring that God had dealt bitterly with her. But as Ruth and Naomi got settled in their new home, Naomi's bitterness apparently began to melt away. We know from various parts of the book of Ruth that Ruth was extremely good to Naomi.

Sometimes, a bitter person needs to be humble enough to receive help, as Naomi did from Ruth. Bitterness isolates people. It makes them say, sometimes viciously, "I don't need your help." As Christians, we are designed to help one another. We are not supposed to be totally independent and self-sufficient. It takes humility to allow someone else to get close enough to help us — and where humility is, bitterness loses ground.

Ruth's kindness to Naomi never waned. She spent her days doing the sweaty, back-breaking work of gleaning in the fields so that she and Naomi would have something to eat. In time, Naomi realized that Ruth had been gleaning in Boaz's field and put two and two together to realize that Ruth might have a future with Boaz. And just like that, Naomi had a cause. She was needed again.

Ruth was a foreigner in Bethlehem. We cannot assume that she knew the local customs. No, she needed Naomi to help her. She needed Naomi to explain Boaz's potential as a member of the family who might be able to marry her, and to tell her what to do to express her interest in him. Perhaps she needed Naomi to help make sure that her clothes looked just right before she went to the threshing floor that evening.

Everything seems to have changed after Naomi realized that she was needed again. Not only did she have a reason to live, she also had hope for the future. Any person who is bitter will benefit from helping others, from having a cause and gaining the opportunity to focus on something besides the self. When the heart begins to turn outward, the flood of bitterness within it begins to recede.

You probably know how Naomi's story ends. Ruth and Boaz did marry, and had a son named Obed. This child was called "a restorer of life" to Naomi (see Ruth 4:15). She became a nurse to him — and he became the grandfather of King David, an ancestor of Jesus Christ. Naomi's latter years were greater than her former days. She knew a kind of joy in her old age that she had not known in her youth.

I believe that an older woman — every seasoned mother, grandmother, and great-grandmother — is a treasure chest for those around her. Within her are jewels of wisdom, maturity, perspective, sound counsel, and encouragement, just to name a few. I call these women "harvest women," for theirs is the unique privilege of bringing in the latter harvest.

My sister, you have something to give to life in your senior years. Your latter days will be glorious. God will restore what you have lost. New life will nurse at the breasts of your wisdom. Your cries have been heard in heaven; your prayers will be answered. Simply make sure that you live your life free of bitterness, so that there is room in your heart to hold all the grand and glorious things God wants to give to you.

Before we conclude, I would like to offer you three suggestions, "weed killers," which, if you take seriously, will enable you to banish any bitterness that may be within you. Oh, I know that you may have to make some adjustments in your thinking in order to apply this advice to your life, but if you do, you will be so glad. Once the bitterness is gone, a whole new life awaits you.

1. EMBRACE THE IDEA THAT GOD IS STILL IN CONTROL.

Most people become bitter when they feel that someone else has "won," that someone else has been given what they wanted or thought they deserved. When people feel cheated or defeated, bitterness begins to worm its way into the soul.

We have to believe that God has a purpose in all things and that His purposes are better for us than anything we could ever imagine for ourselves. Perhaps you remember the biblical story of Joseph. If not, read it in Scripture in Genesis 37–39 and realize that what others intend for our harm, God can use for our good.

God did work out Joseph's situation for good — for his own good and for the good of his family. God wants to do the same for

239

you. Regardless of what you have been through — and I know it may have been horrible — God wants to use it for your benefit. Remember that "all things work together for good to those who love God, to those who are the called according to His purpose" (Romans 8:28). If you love God, you can count on the fact that He will work out even the heartaches and heartbreaks for good.

When you are disappointed or devastated, remember that God is in control, and do not give in to the temptation to become bitter over the developments of your life. I have heard it said that we must trust God's heart when we cannot see His hand. So, when things look bad for you, refuse to be discouraged or angry. Instead, take a deep breath and tell yourself that God is in control and that somehow, everything is going to work out better than you ever dreamed.

2. TALK ABOUT WHAT YOU ARE TEMPTED TO BURY.

People are often tempted to hide the things that are painful to them, the things that could make them appear to be weak or wounded. Some tend to want to bury their hurts and disappointment beneath designer clothes, fast cars, or professional success. Some use silence as a cover-up; others become the life of the party, always hiding their pain behind a clever joke or a funny story. Whatever our "dirt" of choice may be, it will do us harm in the end. Things that are covered with soil eventually take root and grow. Bitterness will do that in the soil of our souls if we allow it to.

The only healthy way to live is to confront the things we would rather bury and to deal with them. If we do not, our hearts will begin to decay like a body in a grave; bitterness will eat at them until there is nothing left.

I can remember my mother often saying that things grow in the dark. When I was a little boy and scraped my knee or cut my finger, she always advised letting air get to my injury. She was not a fan of covering up wounds with bandages or dressings because, well, things — like germs — grow in the dark, causing cuts and scrapes to take longer than necessary to heal.

I think my mother's simple first aid advice applies to the soul as well as it does to the human body. We must allow air and light to touch our wounded places. We cannot cover the wounds of our hearts or all sorts of bad things will grow. No, we have to leave them exposed. I am not suggesting that you broadcast your sob stories to everyone you know, but I do believe that honest conversation with a trusted friend or minister is extremely beneficial to the healing process. Anytime you feel anger, hurt, or disappointment rising up in your heart, do not reach for the shovel to bury it. Instead, run toward the light. Keep it out in the open so that you can deal with it and not grow bitter.

3. MAKE SOMETHING OUT OF THE ROOT.

Any situation or circumstance that could lead to bitterness in your heart has the potential to take root within you. It will not just rest somewhere in your psyche; it *will* grow. This is why the writer of Hebrews refers to the "root of bitterness," as I mentioned earlier in this chapter.

One of the interesting aspects of roots is that, for centuries, they have been used to make medicines. Long before there were prescription antibiotics, drive-through pharmacies, or a Food and Drug Administration, there were roots and leaves and berries that, in the hands of the right people, could be ground or crushed or whittled into salves or poultices to sooth and heal a variety of ailments and infirmities. Many of these natural ingredients were bitter to the taste, but they made people better.

This ever-so-brief and oversimplified history of medicine brings me to an important point: a bitter root has the potential to heal. Something bitter can make something better. Often, bitter roots or herbs are crushed or heated in order to produce a fragrance or oil. In the same way, people who have had negative things happen to them can become a sweet, fragrant healing balm in other people's lives.

The next time an opportunity to allow a root of bitterness to be buried in your heart presents itself, begin to look for ways that it can make you stronger instead. Ask God to heal your hurts, then take the bitterness of that anger, that offense, or that disappointment and turn it into forgiveness, graciousness, or hope. Those things will not only promote healing in your own heart, you will be able to use them to help others too.

I want to remind you that Naomi's bitterness turned to blessing. Her sadness turned to joy. Her empty arms were filled and her life was restored. God can do the same for you, so do not waste another minute of your life harboring bitterness in your heart.

Homework for the heart: How did your mother combat bitterness in her life? What did she experience that might have inclined her toward bitterness? How did her response affect you? How does it affect you still? How do you battle bitterness in your own life? Who do you need to forgive? Who needs to forgive you?

A mother's secret prayer: Dear Lord, please replace the roots of bitterness in my heart with flowers of praise and seeds of gratitude. Help me to be vigilant to remove any traces of bitterness that would seep into my life and poison me. Purify my heart, my Lord, so that I might pass on a legacy of joy and thanksgiving to my children, not bitterness and anger, self-pity and fear. Amen.

SUBSTITUTE TEACHER
LEARNING FROM
DOLORES HAYFORD

Over the years, Jack Hayford has been called "Pastor" by Hollywood royalty, by people of national and international influence, by Christian celebrities, and by many whose names may never appear in lights or on the honor rolls of humanity, but who are equally important to him. If reconciliation is needed, if a tense or volatile situation needs to be defused with tact and grace, if a gap needs to be closed or a bridge needs to be built between people or groups, if balanced innovation is called for, if a problem or an issue demands the uncommon wisdom and the highest integrity — Jack Hayford is your man. He is a pastor to pastors, a leader of leaders, and one of the most respected men I know. He is a Christian statesman of the highest order.

From a tiny congregation, he built a thriving, vibrant church of thousands in Southern California, and after his retirement as senior pastor, he founded a college and a seminary. He also founded the Jack W. Hayford School of Pastoral Nurture — a week-long program during which he and others from his ministry provide practical teaching and offer personal interaction with a group of pastors from many geographical locations, representing a wide variety of theological persuasions. It's hard for me to imagine a pastor who would not jump at the chance to spend a week with the man affectionately known as "Pastor Jack."

After retirement, when many good men would have vigorously embraced the golf course, Dr. Hayford accepted a challenging assignment. I have always known him to be loyal to his denomination, the International Church of the Foursquare Gospel. By 2004, two denominational leaders had resigned as president of the group amid financial troubles. The Foursquare Church needed a man of extraordinary character to take the reins — and they looked no further than their native son, Jack Hayford. He was a natural for the job, and as he assumed his position as president of the denomination, a fresh wind of encouragement blew through the Foursquare churches and members everywhere knew that they were in good hands. He is turning things around and I believe great days are ahead for him and for those he leads.

This extremely busy man has the unique ability to make anyone in his presence feel as though he has all the time in the world and as though they are the most important person on earth. He is also a thorough thinker and a careful orator, a master craftsman with words. He thinks through what he wants to say and how he wants to say it. People chuckle about the fact that he often prefaces his remarks with lengthy preambles, but I say that his famous "forewords" have secured his place in the Christian community as a friend to all. It's practically impossible not to like this man, with his easygoing manner, his dry-as-burnt-toast sense of humor, his wisdom, his optimism, and his humility. The cover of the July 2005 issue of *Christianity Today* features a photo of Hayford, characteristically seated on a stool with his Bible in hand and the headline "Jack Hayford: The Pentecostal Gold Standard." I could not have described him more aptly!

He is a husband of more than fifty years to his dear wife, Anna; he is a father, a grandfather (and he has some stories that will really make you chuckle!), a great-grandfather, an accomplished songwriter, a best-selling author (just one of his terrific books is *How to Live through a Bad Day*), a speaker in great demand, and the executive editor of a well-respected edition of the Bible and Bible study materials that have sold millions. He has already a distinguished and fruitful ministry, but he is not finished yet — and I am keeping an eye on him, eager to be as effective and productive (not to mention as well-loved) in my seventies as he is in his.

Great men do not simply appear out of thin air. No, they are carefully crafted by the hand of God Himself, who uses circumstances, experiences, victories, and disappointments to develop such people over time. More than that, He also uses to a great degree mothers and fathers, aunts and uncles, mentors and heroes. He seems to use mothers a lot, and many times, great men are the products of great mothers. This is true of Jack Hayford. He certainly had a great mother, as you will see in the following pages, and I am delighted that he has been willing to share this remarkable lady with us.

MY MOTHER, DOLORES HAYFORD
Jack Hayford

What a blessing and privilege it is for me to introduce you to the woman who introduced me to the world. Please meet my mother, Dolores Hayford.

Mama was born in Fort Morgan, Colorado, on April 20, 1916, the first of three children of Chauncey and Marguerite Farnsworth. Mama married my daddy — Jack Hayford — on September 28, 1932, shortly after the onset of the Great Depression. They only had enough money for a dime-store ring, but they had enough love to see them through the trials and challenges of nearly forty-seven years of marriage. Three children were born to this union, and all three of us entered Christian ministry. My sister, Luanne, died in 1978 while serving as a missionary in Hong Kong, and my brother, Jim, and I continue to serve in the Foursquare Church — Jim as a pastor in Seattle, Washington, and I as the current president of the International Church of the Foursquare Gospel.

In October 1935, my mother and father both heard and responded to the Gospel of Jesus Christ. This began a walk with God that modeled the life of the Savior to a host of others as they lived out the distinctive graces of their own gifts — Daddy as a sacrificial giver and a tireless worker; Mama as a spiritually discerning counselor and remarkably gifted teacher.

More than anything else I'd like to tell you that you would have loved my mama if you had had the opportunity to meet her in person. Few people who ever met or talked with my mother were not impressed with the substance of her character. Many things could be said to describe her: she was a happy person; a witty person; a loving, caring, servant-hearted person; she was filled with the gift of mercy; and she was a brilliant woman.

Though her formal educational pedigree was unremarkable, her intellect and powers of reason were not. But she was never impressed with herself and she never attempted to impress anyone else. Still, whenever she spoke, people were impressed. She made more than effective contact with her listeners; she made an impact. She was profound in her teaching, yet her practicality gave her words a place to land in hearts and to be lived out in a daily walk with Jesus Christ. Her genuine Christlike spirituality became credible and accessible because of the way she *lived* the life about which she taught.

My mother was no different from many exceptional teachers in that her teaching gift came with a price. True spirituality and the ability to minister effectively through teaching is not the result of study or intellectual action alone. It is the fruit of two additional essentials: humility in an ongoing experience at Jesus' feet and absolute obedience to the Word of God and the Holy Spirit's voice. To be like Mama, ever teaching, always requires first that a person be ever teachable. That quality of being always teachable — correctable and childlike in the presence of God — is unquestionably the greatest lesson my mother taught me — and she taught it right up to the very end of her life.

All of her life Mama simply loved the Lord and demonstrated that devotion in her practical, everyday thoughts and actions. I never lived one day that I did not see her genuinely taking the Lord seriously, caring for those others didn't seem to be willing to take time for, teaching, speaking, writing, and generally "touching people for God" every way she could, even though she never held an official position in public ministry.

Most of all, this delightful woman was a

very good mother. Besides loving Dad with all her heart and keeping our home a happy place to live in, visit, and be around, Mama raised three children. Even though none of us was taught or required to think that being in ministry was a profession superior to any other, all of us yielded our lives to the full-time service of our Lord Jesus Christ and, no matter how you measure it, Mama had something to do with that. She made serving God a practical, sensible, and joyous way of life — something a person would like to do, and help others know how to do as well.

All of us children would give credit to the grace of God for the blessings and privileges of our lives and ministries. But then, we would probably add, "and God worked so much in us through Mama." She prayed for us all with incredible sensitivity and discernment. At times, she even said to me that the Lord had "shown her something," and I realized that God wouldn't let me get away with anything. The Almighty kept telling my mother on me!

My mother raised us God's way, but she didn't do it alone. My dad, who preceded her in death by eighteen years, served in the military as a young man and then became a railroad man for most of my life. Both professions bred a man with a solid mix of authority and responsibility, which were conveyed by a fervor for "doing things right, even when there's no one looking." My siblings and I knew we were loved, and we grew up learning in a house where God's truth was the rule, but His love was the mood. At our house, holy living was made both happy and livable.

I have many stories about special moments of Mama influencing me, such as the time she dreamed that Jesus met her on a darkened hillside where burnt brush had overtaken the lush, vital growth. The words that came to her in that dream were, "Daughter, it is too late for you to be walking among barren places."

Daddy asked her to share this one night after dinner saying, "Honey, tell the kids what you told me about the Lord's message to you through your dream." The impact of her story on me was a sudden recognition that it was time to clean up any rough edges in my own lifestyle, because if God were cautioning my *mom,* whom I considered extremely holy, then we were all in trouble!

I also remember the night I graduated from college. Mama and Daddy had driven from their home in Oakland all the way to Los Angeles, where I attended school. I received much recognition at the ceremony; it was an exciting night and I was thrilled. But I honestly can say, with God as my witness, I did not feel smug or proud or conceited. Why? Because of the way I was raised. Mama raised all of her children to keep everything in perspective. Even at the young age of a college graduate, I knew that honors and accolades were really not that big a deal, even though they were a big deal!

Mama and Daddy left to return home after the graduation ceremony that night. They had been with us a couple of days and, since Daddy liked to drive at night, they headed out about 11:00 p.m. I went and lay on the bed and sobbed and sobbed. I wept because I realized that driving up the road somewhere on Highway 99 from Los Angeles to Oakland were my parents, and that the reason I received all those awards that night had nothing to do with *me;* it had everything to do with *them!*

Then there was the time shortly after I had finished my studies for ministry. I was standing in the kitchen conversing with Mama when she casually turned to me and said, "Son, whatever you do in ministry, never forget one thing: None of us has a corner on truth." I've never forgotten that, and I haven't any idea how that one word of wisdom — gently laid on a young, just-graduated-from-theological-school pastor — has kept me relatively free from petty attitudes toward others and helped me steer clear of provincialism or doctrinaire divisiveness.

But some of the greatest lessons I learned from my mother while she had cancer, which eventually led to her going home to be with the Lord on October 31,1997. Her lessons in suffering and dying proved to be great lessons in living. She made a difference in the way I (and others) live through the way she died. In fact, she taught us how to die in a time when people don't want to learn that lesson. In June of 1997, I prayed and asked the Lord to take my mother home. In response, I sensed Him saying to my heart, "No, you leave Me to raise her up. It's not your business to pray about her going home; I'll take care of that." I learned a new way to pray for Mama, but the Lord also impressed me that her home going would be an extended process through which He wanted to achieve two things: first, He wanted to speak and teach people through Mother's processing of death; and second, He wanted to minister to my mother in some deeply personal ways.

The Lord showed me that Mama's extended pathway would be a means of bringing truth to false ideas people sometimes have about others they see as very mature believers. Many of us are tempted to think that, if someone has been an especially dear or great person, then his or her passage from this world should be obviously choreographed by God as quick and pain-free. This shows up in such well-meaning thoughts and words as, "I don't understand why God would let someone go through this, especially someone as godly and as caring and as loving and as faithful as —" and then they'll name someone like my mother. But my mother would be the first person to challenge that proposition — not simply because she was humble, but because she was honest. She was very real and practical about the stuff our flesh is made of and knew that none of us ever have any justifiable grounds for making demands on God.

Through Mama's illness and death, I and others around her learned that people of soundly rooted, solidly based faith in Jesus — people who know and have experienced the power and grace in their lives — are not guaranteed a storybook ending to their lives. You need to know that if you must endure an extended trial — whether it is a trial in life or a trial leading to death — I believe our Father God wants to say to you that you are no less spiritual and certainly no less loved by Him because you are experiencing difficult or extended ordeals, pain, struggle, or problems. We all need to realize and embrace this reality of our faith. Jesus didn't come to make life easy for us; He came to fill it with meaning. And He didn't die to buy us a temporal Disneyland, a "magic kingdom." Rather, He shed His blood to purchase eternal glory . . . the Father's unshakable kingdom.

The memory of Mama's passing contains a lesson for all of us today in a time when the supposed mercy of a "mercy killing" argues against trust in the *grander* mercies of Almighty God. Remember, His mercies are new *every* morning, even on the most difficult days. His Word reminds us, however intense our pain or struggles may be, they are next to nothing compared with the fuller substance of Heaven's purposes in us for now, and the promises we can rest in forever.

Mama lived in the truth of 2 Corinthians 4:16–18, and she died with its perspective in mind.

Therefore, we do not lose heart. Even though our outward man is perishing, yet the inward man is being renewed day by day. For our light affliction, which is but for a moment, is working for us a far more exceeding and eternal weight of glory, while we do not look at the things which are seen, but at the things which are not seen. For the things which are seen are temporary, but the things which are not seen are eternal.

Regarding my impression that the Lord was going to do some things especially for her and in her as she walked her extended pathway of sickness to death, I found the Lord faithful to do exactly that. About a month after I had prayed and sensed His desire to work in her life, Mama shared some very tender things with me along that line — without even knowing I was hoping and believing God would do such things. One day near mid-July, my wife Anna and I visited Mama in the hospital. She lay on the pillow, looking pensively out the window, and said, "You know, Son . . ." and then she paused. When she spoke again, she said, "I guess I can't say I'm surprised about this report [from the doctor], because the flesh is so formidable a resister to the Father's purpose. But the Lord has been unveiling so many things to me about me!" Her voice rose to emphasize "me," but at the same time, it broke slightly and tears came to her eyes.

Then she began to relate these things God had brought to her mind: feelings of criticism, judgment. As she shared, she was not engaging in self-flagellation, but in godly humiliation in the wake of a *just-now perceived* unworthiness in her own soul. She wept as she spoke of those things, and then she reached out her hand to me and said, "I want to pray with my Pastor." What a gift! I took her hand and she prayed (as best I can remember), thanking God for His infinite patience with her and for revealing to her those things within her of which she had been previously unaware. She asked Him to cleanse her and continue to wash her clean of her faults until He had brought about the image of His Son Jesus Christ in her life. She then told Him how much she wanted to please Him, perfectly, completely, and fully — and closed her prayer by squeezing my hand and saying, "In Jesus' name, amen."

She was silent for a moment, with her eyes closed. But then she opened them, looked at me, and smiled. Somehow her countenance seemed even more beautiful than before. Please don't mistake that observation; it's not just a son's emotion. The Bible teaches that there is an increasing glory that takes place in the lives of the sons and daughters of the living God who submit to the ongoing process that Mama described in her prayer. The Bible also teaches us that God's ultimate purpose is not to simply forgive and take us to heaven, or to save us and provide for our needs, or to help us and get us through life to eternity. Rather, the Father's highest and ultimate purpose (which was also my mother's deepest passion and the motivation of everything she said, did, thought, and served) is described in Romans 8:28–29. That beloved passage, which is so often recalled in times of trial, says so much more than is often noticed: *"And we know that all things work together for good to those who love God, to those who are the called according to His purpose."* But then what many don't notice is that "His purpose" is defined: *"For whom He foreknew, He also predestined to be conformed to the image of His Son."* Being "conformed to the image of His Son" was the quest for Mama. That was the compelling issue not only in her teaching, but in her life.

The lessons I have learned from my mother's life are true because her one objective was to know Jesus in the power of His resurrection and the fellowship of His suffering. Such a depth of acquaintance with the Savior in mirroring His likeness only flows from glory to glory in a person committed to lifelong teachability and sustained by constant childlike correctability before the Father.

I learned from my mother that it isn't the path of endless spankings or tearful living that makes a holy, worthwhile life; it is the process of ever learning that makes a good life and that makes things really count. Being shaped under the touch of Jesus, sculpted into the likeness of Christ, learning to love, learning to live, learning through staying teachable, learning to die. Whether we're skilled to communicate, as Mama was, is not the point. We don't need to be taught in order to become gifted communicators, but we always need to be taught in order to learn to live.

I want to finish writing about the difference my mother made in my life and in the lives of so many others with one final story. It was an evening that will forever remain etched in my memory. On Thursday, October 16, 1997, Anna and I returned home from a trip earlier than planned because of news that Mama had suddenly taken a turn for the worse. When we arrived at Mama's hospital room, we found a roomful of people and a happy atmosphere. Mama was unusually alert, given her circumstances. Without a plan, without urgent phone calls or special arrangements, within the next two hours, family members simply began to gather. No one was called, they just came.

With her family all around her, Mama was in excellent spirits. It was like joy — like a holy electricity — ricocheting around the room. At one point, Mama was laughing and commenting on things that she had only begun to enjoy in recent years. For example, she said, "There were certain things I refused to do earlier in life because I thought they'd hurt me. For instance, somebody told me years ago that it would be better if I didn't put cream in my coffee. And I've gone all this time without cream in my coffee, until just about three months ago. Then I thought, *what difference does it make?*" Then Mama, who happened to be holding a cup of coffee, put some cream in it and said, "It really irritates me that I've missed this all my life!"

She was laughing about that, and then the subject of different foods came up. She looked over at me and she said, "I feel like I would like the taste of an enchilada in my mouth."

With a little twinkling, an impish smile, I asked, "Really?"

She said, "Yes!"

My son and I hopped in the car and returned about half an hour later with a dozen enchiladas and a box of chocolates to go with it. We dished out an enchilada for Mama, who was eating very little at that time. To our surprise, she ate a whole enchilada! When she finished, I said, "Mama, you need to top it off," and I started popping her chocolates. She had chocolates all over her fingers. I'll never forget the faces of the nurses who were watching this menagerie of people and the outright overwhelming fun we were having as a family.

Later, as family members left one by one, Mama fell asleep. It was a full night with the fullness of joy all around. She'd had so much of her family all at once, so much fun in the gathering. And she'd had her fill.

I conclude with that story not only because it's a happy memory for me, but also because it really is a tiny taste of what heaven is like — and what it's going to be like. Mama's illness and death had their physical ordeals; our family had its struggles too. But woven in, through, and beyond the pain and struggles of any family in which

Jesus Christ has been allowed to continually teach and shape people, redemption rides way beyond everything else. And life far, far, far overreaches death. And joy far, far overreaches pain. And the triumph of God's grace overreaches all the things that we are not in ourselves as human beings. The memory of the "Night of the Enchilada" — that great, joyous family evening — points us to the ultimate day, the eternal presence of the Father.

Mama was a dear lady. She made a difference in my life and in the lives of so many others. She *was* a great lady! I loved her — and I still do love her very much!

LESSON THIRTEEN
MAMAS TEACH US TO SET THE STANDARDS HIGH

Perhaps no one has higher standards than a mother for the kind of people she wants her children to associate with, date, and eventually marry. Many mothers have difficulty accepting the prospects that her children bring home and wonder why their babies would settle for someone so beneath them. Whether their perception is accurate or not (and what mother isn't biased in thinking her children always deserve more!), it's usually not such a bad thing for us to learn to set our standards high. As the classic song reminds us, our mamas tell us that we'd better shop around!

So what do we look for in a godly spouse? What should our standard be, including one that is good enough for Mama? As we turn to God's Word, we find several passages that shed light on these questions. Perhaps the Bible's most thorough and popular description of a godly wife is found in Proverbs

31:10–31. These verses are credited to King Lemuel's mother, and while we do not know much about King Lemuel himself, we know from this passage of Scripture that his mother was one savvy lady. As a mother herself, and presumably as a wife too, this woman had some experience. She knew well what her son needed to look for in the woman he would marry, and her advice was worthy of inclusion in the Holy Scriptures. Countless women since King Lemuel's mother have shared her recommendations with their sons and used her words to pray for their future daughters-in-law. Many, many single women have asked God to help them be the kind of wife defined in this passage, and many wives have done their best to apply the wisdom here to their own lives and families.

One of the most important things a good mother does for her sons is to help them know how to choose an excellent wife. Granted, there is many a mother who does not feel that any woman on earth is good enough for the young man she has raised, but if a woman is realistic, she will realize that he must grow up and that he will probably fall in love along the way. Her job, then, is to teach him what to look for and what to value in a woman. He is likely smart enough to value her youth, her beauty, her flowing hair, and her taut skin while she is young, but he may need some help perceiving what will be valuable in a woman ten, twenty, forty, and fifty years down the road. He needs to know how to look beyond a woman's body down to the pit of her soul, to see the character beneath her curves and the substance beneath her style.

I believe, if you are raising sons, that you desire for them to be great men. You certainly are not longing for them to be mediocre employees, lousy athletes, or ho-hum human beings. Let me tell you something: a great man needs a great woman. Any man with a great mother will have high expectations of his wife — and that is as it should be. I treat my wife well because I would not abuse my mother. It's just that simple.

The bond between a mother and her son is amazing. You can see it around you often. My own mother's advice shaped me in business, in faith, and even in choosing a wife. Now I watch my sons being affected by their mother's opinion. They, even more than their sisters with young men, want to know what Mom thinks of the girl they are seeing, while my daughters bring the guys around me with a bottle of smelling salts, knowing I almost faint when I see them.

My wife, on the other hand, is careful about young girls, I think, and who the boys date. I think that is because women tend to see things in each other that a man would let slide. In fact, men can be blind about women and we do benefit greatly from solicited advice from a wise mother, especially when it comes to the details we do not see.

I hope that you will read this chapter carefully. It is for all kinds of women, not simply for mothers who want to their sons to marry well. If you are a single woman, these verses offer time-tested, proven advice that will enable you to be a blessing to the husband God may bring you. If you are a brand-new bride, these words can help build a strong foundation for the marriage you have just begun to build. If you are a woman who has tried so many different ways to please your man and still find yourself frustrated at the end of every day, this chapter is for you. If you simply need a refresher course in being a wife, I believe this depiction of a godly wife will be just the reminder you need. If you are a grandmother or a great-grandmother, these are wonderful words to pray for the generations after you as they grow up and choose marriage partners.

I would like us to take a close look at this

lady whom the Bible never names, but upon whom many titles have been bestowed, such as "the Proverbs 31 Woman," "the Virtuous Woman," and "the Excellent Wife." The verses describing her are printed here and I hope you will take a moment to read them and savor their richness before we move on.

Who can find a virtuous wife?
For her worth is far above rubies.
The heart of her husband safely trusts her;
So he will have no lack of gain.
She does him good and not evil
All the days of her life.
She seeks wool and flax,
And willingly works with her hands.
She is like the merchant ships,
She brings her food from afar.
She also rises while it is yet night,
And provides food for her household,
And a portion for her maidservants.
She considers a field and buys it;
From her profits she plants a vineyard.
She girds herself with strength
And strengthens her arms.
She perceives that her merchandise is
    good,
And her lamp does not go out by night.
She stretches out her hands to the distaff,
And her hand holds the spindle.

She extends her hand to the poor,
Yes, she reaches out her hands to the
    needy.
She is not afraid of snow for her house-
    hold,
For all her household is clothed with scar-
    let.
She makes tapestry for herself;
Her clothing is fine linen and purple.
Her husband is known in the gates,
When he sits among the elders of the land.
She makes linen garments and sells them,
And supplies sashes for the merchants.
Strength and honor are her clothing;
She shall rejoice in time to come.
She opens her mouth with wisdom,
And on her tongue is the law of kindness.
She watches over the ways of her house-
    hold,
And does not eat the bread of idleness.
Her children rise up and call her blessed;
Her husband also, and he praises her:
"Many daughters have done well,
But you excel them all."
Charm is deceitful and beauty is passing,
But a woman who fears the LORD, she
    shall be praised.
Give her of the fruit of her hands,

And let her own works praise her in the
gates.

(Proverbs 31:10–31)

You will notice that this passage opens with
a question. King Lemuel's mother asks,
"Who can find a virtuous wife? For her
worth is far above rubies." This woman
knew what most of us parents come to find
out — that a virtuous wife does not just appear out of thin air. If you want your son to
have a virtuous wife, or if you want to be
one yourself, you must know that such a
woman indeed must be found. She is like
the fairest flower in the most exquisite
garden. She has been planted in a safe place
by God Himself, nurtured in the rich soil of
His Word, and watered by His love. He has
tended her carefully all of her life and
designed each of her experiences to contribute to her nobility. She is indeed more precious than rubies or emeralds or diamonds
— and, like those costly gems, she is not on
display in a dime store.

No, indeed, a virtuous wife is a treasure.
As a mother, tell your sons to search diligently for her and not to settle for a plastic
rose or a synthetic stone. As a woman, do
not make yourself available to every man
who appears interested. Treat yourself as

the treasure that you are and demand — not with a sharp tongue, but with the force of your virtue and your character and your presentation — that a man who is truly interested in you treat you with equal honor.

My mother told me that the quickest way to surmise what a daughter will be like as she grows older is to observe her mother. While I know that this is not true in every case, it can be a good barometer of values and expectations in that particular family. In my case, I looked at my mother-in-law and thought, *I could live with that!* My wife has turned out to be a tremendous asset to me and our children. Oddly, now I notice my sons trying to find young girls who are like their mother.

Sometimes, it isn't just what you say that influences your children, it is also the way you handle the ones you love and adore. In my sons' case, I think they have ideals about male-female relationships that are largely based on their mother and her treatment of me. I have also seen my wife have to take them into a corner and challenge them about who they are seeing and why. Her words are powerful; her example is extremely comprehensive and it drives them to find certain qualities that are important to them.

Now, let's look back at King Lemuel's mother. After making her point about the value of a virtuous wife, this wise woman immediately moves to a point that I do not think we can emphasize enough. She says: "The heart of her husband safely trusts her; so he will have no lack of gain. She does him good and not evil all the days of her life" (Proverbs 31:11–12).

I believe one of a wife's greatest aspirations should be for her husband's heart to safely trust her — and when it does, it should be her most prized possession. You see, a man's world is often full of distrust and his heart tends toward hesitancy and hiding. He is rarely sure whom he can trust in the workplace or on the ball field. He is careful with his confidences and will not share them with a person he knows will not honor them. Whether he ever lets a woman know it or not, he desperately needs someone who is safe for him. The world is a threatening place; it reminds him often of his weakness and at times, it can cause him to fear. He needs a fortress in which to unload his feelings and his fears. He needs to know that they will not be used against him, but that everything about his heart is safe, treasured, and well-guarded in his wife. For further insights into a man's need to trust and feel safe, I suggest you read my book, *The Lady, Her Lover and Her Lord* and pay particular attention to chapters eight, ten, and eleven.

One of the ways a woman builds and maintains a man's trust is to do him good. That sounds so simple, I know. But let me be frank for a moment. I have been a pastor for nearly thirty years at the time of this writing. I have met some of the finest women on earth. I have done my best to minister to women in ways that are effective and empowering, and my heart has soared as I have seen women healed and set free by the power of God and as I have watched them take their places as leading ladies upon the stage of life. But I must tell you that I have also crossed paths with women who are so broken, so angry, so jealous, so manipulative, so vindictive, and so vengeful that there is no way they would do any man anything but evil; they simply are not equipped emotionally to do good. Now, I do understand why these women are the way they are; much of my ministry has been devoted to their healing and restoration. I wholeheartedly believe that God wants to make them whole and strong. But unless and until they let the Great Potter touch their broken hearts, they will only get worse.

I suspect that King Lemuel's mother had encountered such women too. Otherwise, she would not have mentioned a woman's potential to do harm. Let me encourage mothers of sons to tell your young men to beware of an angry woman or a controlling woman. Tell him that jealousy is not cute and that manipulating other people is not a game. Let him know that if he touches her emotions in a way that is appropriate and godly and feels a jagged edge, she may be a broken vessel. Encourage him to seek a lady who has a whole heart, steady emotions, and a sound mind.

A woman needs to be predisposed to do her husband good. That comes from a pure heart, a whole heart. It is instinctive, not forced, and it is a treasure unlike any other to be found in a wife.

King Lemuel's mother knew that there are also practical aspects to being an excellent wife. Her first jewels of advice are critical, but a virtuous woman does not stop with them. No, a woman who seeks to follow the Proverbs 31 model works with a willing heart and is diligent, wise, and caring. She is a good boss; she has good business sense, manages money well, makes smart investments, constantly looks to improve her skills, knows her value and the value of her work, and labors at a task until it is complete. She does not ignore the plight of the needy, but gives from her resources. The woman sounds bionic! Look at the Bible's description of the work ethic she possesses and the variety of her skills, on top of her ability to provide for her family and for her servants.

She seeks wool and flax,
And willingly works with her hands.
She is like the merchant ships,
She brings her food from afar.
She also rises while it is yet night,
And provides food for her household,
And a portion for her maidservants.
She considers a field and buys it;
From her profits she plants a vineyard.
She girds herself with strength,
And strengthens her arms.
She perceives that her merchandise is
    good,
And her lamp does not go out by night.
She stretches out her hands to the distaff,
And her hand holds the spindle.
She extends her hand to the poor,
Yes, she reaches out her hands to the
    needy.
                        (Proverbs 31:13–20)

I believe that this passage applies equally to women who have professional careers and to women who do their work primarily at home. Whether a woman employs her diligence, savvy, and skill in the marketplace or within the four walls of her home, she needs to embrace opportunities to maximize the gifts and talents within her, contribute to the good of others, and have a healthy evaluation of who she is and what she does.

Every woman must have a strong and vibrant spiritual life to uphold her natural life. Personally, I believe that the next several verses refer to a woman's relationship with God. In Proverbs 31:21–23 we read: "She is not afraid of snow for her household, for all her household is clothed with scarlet. She makes tapestry for herself; her clothing is fine linen and purple." I still believe what I have said before: the scarlet garments that cover the virtuous woman's family represent and foreshadow the blood of Christ, which cleanses us and protects us.

I also believe that the "fine linen and purple" in which the woman is arrayed symbolizes royalty. She is indeed a daughter of the King. She lives in communion with the King of kings. She is secure in her position in Him, and she is not afraid to show it. In addition, "strength and honor are her clothing; she shall rejoice in time to come" (Proverbs 31:25). This woman is fully clothed in the boldness that comes from knowing God. I think that is the only way she can rejoice in the days ahead of her. She knows that she is strong enough to face whatever comes her way.

In Proverbs 31:23–29, we see again her industrious side and her business abilities. We also see that she speaks words of wisdom and kindness. We also catch a glimpse of the virtuous woman's husband. He is "known in the gates, when he sits among the elders of the land" (Proverbs 31:23). In other words, he is a man of prominence. Others respect and honor him. That's the kind of man a virtuous woman chooses as her covenant partner. Along with her children, he calls her blessed and he praises her above all others. "Many daughters have done well," he says, "but you excel them all" (Proverbs 31:29).

As King Lemuel's mother brings her description of a virtuous woman to a close, she says: "Charm is deceitful and beauty is passing, but a woman who fears the LORD, she shall be praised. Give her of the fruit of her hands, and let her own works praise her in the gates" (Proverbs 31:30–31). Charm may fascinate a man for a moment, but it does not indicate character in a woman. Beauty may turn a man's head for a while, but eventually, hair goes gray, body parts seem to shift a bit, wrinkles appear, teeth fall out. True, lasting beauty is found inside — and a great man is always able to see it in the woman he loves.

I can assure you that nothing is as attractive in a woman as the fear of the Lord. Knowing God, honoring God, and worshipping God are really the most praiseworthy endeavors a person can ever undertake. And a woman who knows how to talk to Him and hear from Him is a force of strength and beauty like no other. Nothing makes a lady more radiant than spending time in His presence. That's where the true prize is.

To you women who are raising sons to be husbands to excellent wives someday, I say: tell those boys to set their standards high. And to those of you who are wives already or will be someday: take the advice of King Lemuel's mother. You *can* be the kind of woman she describes. It will require choices and discipline, but it is certainly possible for you. This excellent mother's words are ancient indeed, but they are timeless in their truth and proven in their wisdom.

Homework for the heart: What did you learn from your mother about setting the standards high? How did she typically respond to your dates and boyfriends? How have you pursued being like the Proverbs 31 woman? In what areas do you need the most growth? How are you pursuing that growth? Set a realistic goal for this week and then follow through on accomplishing it.

A mother's secret prayer: Dear God, I pray that I may exemplify the kind of woman that King Lemuel's mother describes in Proverbs, not perfect by any means, but empowered by You to be all that I can be. I ask that my sons find wives with these qualities and that my daughters pursue the excellence of actions and integrity of character that You want us to display. Help us to keep our standards high. Amen.

LESSON FOURTEEN
MAMAS TEACH US THAT LOVE HAS THE LAST LAUGH

The Bible says: "Hope deferred makes the heart sick" (Proverbs 13:12). Time can wear down your patience and numb you to the dreams that you hold so dear. Have you ever started out believing in God to do something in your life and then waited and waited until finally you said to yourself, "This is not going to happen"? Assuming it is a God-given vision (and not your own flight of fancy), it doesn't mean that because it didn't happen quickly, it will not come to pass. Like childbirth, the birthing of a dream or promise takes longer than you might expect. I have met few pregnant women who were happy by their ninth month! Generally, they are tired of waiting, heavy with child, and ready to rid themselves of the burden they bear. This business of waiting on God is not for the weak!

No, it takes strength to maintain your intensity even when the vision has been a long time coming to pass. As I write to you today, I have the distinct feeling of being used of God to encourage a mother in waiting to hold on to her dream. I am not only addressing a mother who is waiting for a child, though that would be nice — but maybe a mother who is waiting on a child to get saved or a mother who is waiting on a thirty-something son to mature. Mothers often have to wait through tough things. Do not give up, though. Help is on the way!

As I think about the things you may be waiting for, I am reminded of a woman in the Bible. She wanted a child, but she thought it would never happen. She was not unreasonable; she simply knew that a woman's chances of conceiving and bearing a child after age seventy were nonexistent.

She was among the barren, among the likes of Rachel, Hannah, and Elizabeth — good, godly women whose most desperate longings eluded them. She was among the childless and because of her age, she also seemed to be among the hopeless.

Her name was Sarai, until God changed it to Sarah after a life-changing spiritual encounter. She was the wife of Abram, later Abraham, one of the greatest men of faith who ever lived and one of the very few ever referred to as the "friend of God" (see

James 2:23). We know that Abraham was a wealthy man and that Sarai was extremely attractive, but riches and beauty could not satisfy their longing for a child or fill the gaping, baby-shaped hole in their hearts.

God knew how desperately they wanted an heir, as God always knows the desperate desires of His people. Though the years had thoroughly convinced Abram and Sarai that children were impossible, God had a different plan. He appeared to Abram in a vision and promised him that "one who will come from your own body shall be your heir" (Genesis 15:4). As if that were not enough of a surprise, God then led Abram outside, under the clear desert night sky, and said: " 'Look now toward heaven, and count the stars if you are able to number them.' And He said to him, 'So shall your descendants be' " (Genesis 15:5).

I want to call your attention to Abram's response to God's promise, for it is the response that you must embrace if you want to experience the fulfillment of God's promises in your life. The Bible tells us that Abram "believed in the LORD, and He accounted it to him for righteousness" (Genesis 15:6). When God makes you a promise, you must believe. You must believe that He has spoken, no matter how unlikely the fulfillment of His word may seem, and you must believe in His desire and ability to bring fulfillment, no matter what obstacles exist. More often than not, there will be times of testing and even of contending as you await the fulfillment of God's word to you. You may fight the enemies of discouragement in your own soul, negative comments from other people, or a series of circumstances that seem to hinder your dream rather than help it on its way. In order to pass the tests and win the victory, faith is essential. You may have to stand in faith against more formidable challenges than you ever imagined, and you may have to cling to your faith for longer than you would like, but do not grow weary or discouraged. Keep the faith. Practice a relentless belief in God, in His promise, and in the fact that He will perform His promise. He is faithful, so no matter how long it takes, refuse to give up on Him.

Unfortunately, Sarai's wait got the better of her. She grew tired of waiting on God. After all, she had been waiting for a child for more than eighty years — and that is a *long* time. We have all been tempted to take matters into our own hands when the delay of God's promises becomes unbearable. We have all begun to wonder whether we even heard Him speak to us at all. Maybe the force of desperation in our deep desires caused us think it was God, we reason. Maybe we were hearing the seductive whispers of our souls instead of the clear sound of our Father's voice. "Maybe it was not God after all," we say to ourselves. Such comments, even when spoken only to your own soul, are seeds of doubt — and, left untended, they will spring forth into full-grown weeds of unbelief that will overtake the faith you have so diligently cultivated in your heart.

Disappointment, delay, and the dwindling of faith can drive us to take the most unwise actions, but we must remember, as the saying goes, "God's delays are not God's denials." When Sarai's patience ran out, she did something extremely dangerous. She gave up on God. I can only imagine her crying and screaming in frustration or slamming her fist and stomping her feet in fury and grief as she decided that God was not going to fulfill His promise to her. I am sure she was angry; she probably felt she had been "had," and she was likely devastated because she had sacrificed so much in order for Abram to follow God and she had believed so deeply in Him herself. She had to have known in her heart that He was indeed faithful, and yet circumstances indicated otherwise. She had waited on Him too long, she reasoned, so she decided to take matters into her own hands. We need to realize that only one person can be in control of the situations in our lives: either God or us. If you or I decide to commandeer a situation, God will allow us to do so. But if we say that we trust Him, then we must keep our hands off and wait patiently and expectantly for Him to fulfill His promise.

It is dangerous to take matters into your own hands. I know how tempting it is to help God bless you, but, in reality, He does not need your help to bless you and He does not need your help to protect you. He is quite capable of seeing you through. All God needs from you is the strength to persevere and wait. Impatience can make matters much worse. How many times have you spoken too soon and wished you had waited to speak your mind? I know that many times we resolve things so that we can get on with our lives — only to find out that we delayed something positive by getting in God's way. I know Sarai wished she had kept quiet. But, oh no! She had to get involved in it and ended up complicating her own blessing and needlessly hurting people in the process. Have you been there? I have.

What Sarai did, in her despair and impatience, was to send Abram to her maid, Hagar, thinking that Abram's promised son might not be the fruit of her aged womb after all. She must have known that a man's fertility exceeds a woman's and that if she specifically recalled God's promise, He had made it to Abram, with no mention of her. When Abram paid his conjugal visit to Hagar, she became pregnant. Instead of satisfying Sarai, this development made her angry and miserable. I wonder, sometimes, if she was secretly hoping her scheme with Hagar would fail, wanting God to prove Himself to her by diverting nature's course in Abram's relations with Hagar and showing her that nothing she could do would thwart His promise. But He did not. He sat back and allowed biology to have its way, thereby also allowing Sarai to have her way. She realized that her way led to nothing but trouble — not only to strife and anger between Hagar and Sarai, but a lifetime of animosity between Isaac and Ishmael and violence between their descendants.

What happened with Sarai is no different from what happens when you and I grab the reins of our lives. When we insist upon imposing human effort, human reasoning, and human timing onto the promises of God, He may allow us to do so in order that we may see how faulty our own plans and pursuits really are. In many cases, people who run ahead of God, refusing to wait on Him and taking control of their circumstances themselves, end up with a price to pay. Of course, God forgives, but there are consequences for turning up one's nose at Him. In Sarai's case, it was Hagar's son, Ishmael. In other situations, it could be a missed opportunity that would have been a great blessing if you had only waited. It could be a bad marriage instead of the happy union God wanted to give you if you had simply given Him a few more months. It could be a situation of overwhelming debt instead of the financial freedom you would have enjoyed had you only waited until you could pay cash. Let me assure you: when God asks you to wait for something, it is best to obey, no matter how desperately you want to make it happen for yourself.

Sarai's refusal to wait on God did not change His promise. His promises always stand, no matter how we interfere. He appeared to Abram again, when Abram was ninety-nine years old, and affirmed His promise, saying:

As for Me, behold, My covenant is with you, and you shall be a father of many nations. No longer shall your name be called Abram, but your name shall be Abraham; for I have made you a father of many nations. I will make you exceedingly fruitful; and I will make nations of you, and kings shall come from you. And I will establish My covenant between Me and you and your descendants after you in their generations, for an everlasting covenant, to be God to you and your descendants after you. (Genesis 17:4–7)

God went on to clarify His promise, saying specifically: "As for Sarai your wife, you shall not call her name Sarai, but Sarah shall be her name. And I will bless her and also give you a son by her; then I will bless her, and she shall be a mother of nations; kings of peoples shall be from her. . . . My covenant I will establish with Isaac, whom Sarah shall bear to you at this set time next year" (Genesis 17:15–16, 22).

Later, the Lord visited Abraham again, and the Bible tells us that Sarah eavesdropped on their conversation and heard Him say: "I will certainly return to you according to the time of life, and behold, Sarah your wife shall have a son" (Genesis

18:10). Her response? She "laughed within herself, saying, 'After I have grown old, shall I have pleasure, my lord being old also?' " (Genesis 18:12).

God delights to surprise us. He loves to hear the sound of our laughter when it is the joyous overflow of a happy heart or the gentle chuckle that accompanies the sweetness of fulfillment. There are times when we laugh *with* Him, but we dare not laugh *at* Him or at His word. God did not let Sarah get away with her laughter, but said to Abraham, " 'Why did Sarah laugh, saying, 'Shall I surely bear a child, since I am old?' Is anything too hard for the LORD? At the appointed time I will return to you, according to the time of life, and Sarah shall have a son.' " But Sarah denied it, saying, " 'I did not laugh,' for she was afraid. And He said, 'No, but you did laugh!' " (Genesis 18:13–15).

The idea that she would conceive — with her teeth falling out, her sagging breasts, her gray hair, and her wrinkled skin, was so ridiculous to her that she could not help but laugh. The thought that she could conceive at her age was, well, inconceivable! But she needed to know, just as you and I need to know, that our God is the God of the impossible. He is a miracle-working

God who will not be restricted by time or circumstance. He will cause barren wombs to bear children; He will cause dead desires to burst into glorious fulfillment; He will resurrect discarded dreams and, sometimes at the most impossible and surprising moment, fulfill hopes that have been held for a lifetime. This is what He did for Abraham and Sarah.

God is going to make you laugh too. Now that is no big deal for some of you. You have had joy all your life. But there are some who have gone through so much that you are not laughing anymore. Life has dealt you some tough blows and now you find yourself empty and depleted. But when God makes us laugh, it is often because we have been through so much that the idea of getting a blessing like that at a time like this — well, it is hilarious. That is what the joy of the Lord is all about — ridiculous testimonies, the kind that give you joy every time you think about them.

It is not too late for you to laugh again. Maybe the enemy has stolen your joy, but this is your chance to regain it. I am not talking about the laughter you laugh to entertain people or to please them or the laughter that camouflages your disappointment. I mean that deep-down laughter that comes from a merry heart. That is what God wants for you. That is what you are going to have when all is said and done.

That is what Abraham and Sarah ended up with and Genesis 21:1–7 reveals the grand finale of God's promise to them.

> And the LORD visited Sarah as He had said, and the LORD did for Sarah as He had spoken. For Sarah conceived and bore Abraham a son in his old age, at the set time of which God had spoken to him. And Abraham called the name of his son who was born to him — whom Sarah bore to him — Isaac. Then Abraham circumcised his son Isaac when he was eight days old, as God had commanded him. Now Abraham was one hundred years old when his son Isaac was born to him. And Sarah said, "God has made me laugh, and all who hear will laugh with me." She also said, "Who would have said to Abraham that Sarah would nurse children? For I have borne him a son in his old age."

Note that God "visited Sarah as He had said," and that He "did for Sarah as He had spoken" (Genesis 21:1). I want you wrap your heart around those words for yourself right now. I say to you that God will visit you as He has said. He will do for you as He has promised. Your fulfillment may not come when you want it to or when you think it should, but it will come. Your job is to believe, and then to wait with hope and expectation.

You may be saying, as I have said, "God, you have all the time in the world. You are eternal, but I am temporal and frankly, I am running out of time!" But don't you see that God knows that better than we do? He even knows exactly how many hairs are on our heads. Surely, you know that God knows better than you do how much time you have and what season it is in your life. Let me tell you that it does not have to be harvest time for you to bear fruit. All the conditions do not necessarily have to be right for God to perform His work in your life. In fact, sometimes I think God waits on purpose so that all of your enemies and naysayers can see how evident He is in your life. Lazarus was in the grave four days before Jesus called him to come out and he emerged alive. The best wine was served at the end of the wedding (see John 2:1–10). The man at the pool was healed without an angel troubling the waters (see John 5:1–9). And Sarah had her child when she was old. It is never too late for God to intervene.

My sister, let me remind you that God's timing is perfect. He has His reasons for taking His own sweet time. Even when you can hardly wait, when you think you may burst wide open if you have to wait another minute, God is patiently orchestrating every aspect of your desire, arranging every piece of it in perfect order, making sure all the people and places and things involved are at their peak of preparation. Like a seasoned maestro conducting an intricate symphony, He knows just when to bring in each instrument that is needed to make the richest and most perfect sound out of your life. His foot is tapping the beat that is best for you. What seems hopelessly late to you is precisely on schedule to Him. His promises to you *will* come to pass in the best possible time and the best possible way. Do not doubt, question, or despair when you encounter a delay. Most of all, do not take matters into your own hands. You do not want a promise prematurely; you do not want to cheapen something God wants to give you by going out and getting it on your own strength.

Do not give up on God; do not grow weary as you wait for Him to fulfill His promise to you, no matter how late the hour may seem, no matter how impossible the circumstances may appear. Whether impossibility presents itself in the form of your physical age, your absence of experience, your shortage of funds, or your lack of support, you must remember that all things are possible when you believe. What God has said, He will do. Nothing is too hard for Him, and He is good for His word. And you, like Sarah, *will* hold your promise in your arms.

Get ready, get ready, get ready. Warm the milk, wash the pacifier, fold the receiving blanket — because when God blesses you, it will be too late to prepare. Now is the time to get ready for the greatest season in your life. Yes, Sarah learned that God often does His greatest work when you have decided that it is too late. Prepare for what He has promised, for you do not have much time. The miracle is on its way and the preparations should be in place. Your dream is about to be born!

Homework for the heart: Can you think of a dream of your mother's that took a long time to be realized? How did she respond during the process of birthing this dream? What are the dreams that you are still waiting on God to bring to fruition? What can you do during this waiting period to prepare yourself for their actualization?

A mother's secret prayer: Oh, Lord, You know the secret desires of my heart and the dreams that You alone have planted there. I pray that I will continue hoping and trusting, just like Sarah, even when the dream seems impossible, until that day when the dream is birthed and Your love has the last laugh. Give me patience along the way and peace in the waiting. Amen.

■ ■ ■ ■

Part Three
Graduation Day:
Lessons on Longevity from Our Greatest Teachers

■ ■ ■ ■

When my mother-in-law, Virginia Jamison (whom you met in our first section), was in the hospital at the end of her life, I took my mother to visit her. The two had become friends, of course, united by their children's family and the grandchildren between them, not to mention the other facets of their lives that they shared in common. By the time Mama and I made it up to Mrs. Jamison's room, she was breathing with a ventilator along with an assortment of other medical machinery and paraphernalia. The place smelled like most hospitals, with that antiseptic scent laced with an assortment of bodily odors and medicinal aromas. The lighting was dim and the place somber and even a bit morbid feeling. I questioned my judgment in bringing my own ailing mother to such a place even though she had insisted on seeing her friend again.

Inside Mrs. Jamison's room, her children

and grandchildren had gathered quietly around her, listening intently to her labored, and mechanically enhanced, breathing. Mrs. Jamison fluttered her eyes toward us and Mama headed right over to her and clasped her hand. She looked around the room and then down into the eyes of this woman, whose life was similar to hers in so many various ways.

"You must be a happy woman!" my mother exclaimed, beaming down at her peer.

Now I confess for a brief moment that I felt just a little embarrassed and wondered how in the world my mother could make such a statement to this poor woman on her deathbed. Mrs. Jamison, however, clearly met my mother's eyes and nodded in approval. My mother continued, "You must be a happy woman. You got all your children gathered around your bed." Then the two women's eyes continued a silent conversation, a mutual acknowledgment of the full and joyous life that Mrs. Jamison was now drawing to a peaceful close. And in those moments, the mood shifted in the room and the shadows of grief and sorrow became infiltrated with shafts of light, the illuminating joy of a life well-lived and a family celebrating its loving matriarch.

You see, it took my mother to recognize the richness of a life fully lived. Where I along with the others saw only sadness, my mother clarified the process of dying as a spectacular close to a long and fruitful life. I've held that scene in my mind's eye many times since, reflecting on how my mother persevered through so much of her life and what she taught me about pressing on even when the tide of events around me threatens to pull me under.

What is the secret of longevity, of perseverance and pushing onward and upward? How do we keep the faith when the night is pitch black and there isn't a speck of a star to guide us? When we feel betrayed and belittled, burdened and bedraggled? I believe that the lessons our mothers teach us, more than any others, reveal how we not only survive life's hardships and happenings but how we thrive in the midst of them. In Hebrews, Paul exhorts us to run the race set before us and not grow weary, to view the prize at the end as more than worthy of all our efforts and advances. A great cloud of witnesses, the saints of our Christian faith, surround the sidelines cheering us on. I have no doubt who stands at the forefront of that group in my race. With the lessons of their lives, our mamas teach us to never give up our spirit of hope and endurance, and with our heavenly destination in mind, to enjoy every step along the way.

LESSON FIFTEEN
MAMAS TEACH US TO ENDURE

There are many building blocks in the foundation of longevity, but certainly one of the cornerstones is endurance. In fact, one of the greatest lessons my mother ever taught me was to endure. That may not sound particularly profound to you, but let me remind you that endurance is the foundation of success. If we do not endure, we do not succeed. Endurance is a step beyond survival; it is not all the way to triumph — but we cannot triumph without it. To endure is the very best we can do at certain times, under certain circumstances.

The fact that billions of people are alive and well all over the world today is due to the endurance of their ancestors. Had our progenitors given up, you and I would not be here today. Had they failed to persevere through difficult days, we would never have drawn our first breath.

Mothers have a history of endurance. In

the United States alone, over the brief two hundred or so years that our country has been in existence and during the previous years when Native Americans roamed the land before the first settlers ever arrived, mothers endured the threats of wild animals, the rigors of blazing trails through virgin territories, the challenges of building houses and making homes from scratch, the complex establishment of a new nation and an emotionally charged Revolutionary War in which they lost their husbands, sons, and brothers. They have endured the utter degradation and toil of slavery and a violent Civil War, in which some of them tasted freedom for the first time in their lives. They have endured not being able to vote — when many of them had more sense than some of the men! They have endured World War I, again sacrificing the men and boys they loved with all their hearts on soil they would never see. They have endured the Great Depression — a time that demanded wisdom, fortitude, courage, and sacrifice beyond anything my generation has ever known. They have endured the Second World War, when they practically kept the United States running because so many men were abroad. Had it not been for the mothers, factories would have closed, shipments would have ceased, and morale would have sunk to a point beyond recovery. They have endured the vile injustice of segregation and the valiant fight for civil rights. They have endured the losses of more husbands, sons, and brothers in Korea and Vietnam, the World Trade Center, the Pentagon, Pennsylvania, Afghanistan, and Iraq.

The mothers of America — and likewise, mothers all over the world — have indeed persevered through heartache and heartbreak, through fears and tears, through lean times and lack. They have done it because there is something in their hearts that refuses to give up, no matter how fierce the challenge. If there is one thing a mother is not, it's a quitter. No, a mother will persevere for the sake of those she loves through the greatest of difficulties. She will scale the most rugged of mountains, leap the highest of obstacles, and keep walking through the darkest of nights because of her love for her children.

For, you see, a woman's children are her hope and her future. Through them she will accomplish things she could not do herself; she will fulfill dreams that somehow slipped through her own fingers. Her children do not carry her DNA, they carry her heart into days that she will never live and into places she will never go. Through them, her life goes on when her heart has stopped beating. For that reason, and for all the hopes and dreams she has for them, she will endure just about anything.

Perhaps the greatest challenge of endurance I ever saw my own mother face took place over a long period of time. As I have shared, my father developed kidney disease when I was about ten years old and suffered with it until he died when I was sixteen. Before he became ill, he had owned his own business and been a good provider for our family. He had been a strong, strapping, able-bodied man who was gradually reduced to a mere shell of a person. As his illness took its toll on him over time, it also presented my mother with a variety of challenges.

My mother's job became our primary means of support, and she knew that her own future provision and the provision for our family now rested upon her shoulders. Where she had been able to share that burden with my father, it now became hers to bear alone. In addition, there were the bills and needs that illness always brings and there were the everyday duties of taking care of a sick person. Holding down a full-time job, mothering a son like me (my older siblings had moved away from home by this time), and caring for a sick husband for six years will develop endurance in anybody!

I did everything I could to help my mother during those days and I learned so much from her. I learned that endurance is not about being happy; endurance is about being faithful and it is about sacrifice. Maybe that's what endurance really is, after all — day-after-day faithfulness to sacrifice what we need or want in order to focus on surviving a difficult situation and helping others do the same. I was a typical young man who wanted to be riding his bicycle and shooting basketball with the other boys in the neighborhood. Instead, my daily duties included feeding and bathing my father, changing his bed, and being intimately acquainted with a dialysis machine.

My mother had her own responsibilities during those days — some of them similar to mine: preparing his meals, washing him, keeping his environment clean, making sure we had the medical supplies he needed. I think now of how difficult it must have been for her to stay through my father's illness. This gifted, talented, determined, capable woman could have easily left; she could have spent her days enjoying her life and pursuing her passions instead of cleaning up after a man who would never be able to repay her and could hardly manage to thank her. But she stayed; she rose to the challenges every day for six years; she endured. And through her endurance, she taught me to be unselfish. She certainly did not need anything from my father, and in his condition he had nothing to offer but need. But she firmly believed that my siblings and I needed a male influence in our lives, even though illness had robbed him, and us, of his strength and vitality.

Even though I wanted him to, I knew my father would not last forever. We could see the life leaving him one day at a time. There came a time when I knew that, someday, sooner rather than later, he would be gone — and Mom and me, well, we would have endured. When we had endured, we would go on.

The great scholar known as the Apostle Paul wrote a letter to the Christians in Rome around AD 56. Those words, though they are centuries old, were applicable more than thirty years ago as my mother endured my father's illness and death, and they are just as relevant to you today, no matter what you are having to endure. He wrote: "we also glory in tribulations, knowing that tribulation produces perseverance; and perseverance, character; and character, hope" (Romans 5:3–4).

Perseverance (which is just another word for endurance) through suffering was not easy for my mother and it was not easy for me. But it did produce and refine character in us, and it indeed gave us hope. Because of what we endured during those days, we were hopeful and confident in the face of every trial to follow. Because we knew we *could* endure, we always knew we *would* endure.

I want you to know that you, too, can endure anything you are up against right now. Oh, I know that it may take quite some time; endurance cannot be rushed. And I know that it will not be easy; endurance rarely is. It will not be fun, either; but it will develop character and strength in you that fun is not designed to accomplish. When you are faced with a situation to endure, ease is not your goal. Your aim is to keep putting one foot in front of the other as you walk through the winds of adversity, even as they howl around you and threaten to knock you down. The seasons of life that require you to endure and refuse to quit are the times when wisdom, courage, fortitude, and faith are nourished in your soul. Without them, you cannot fulfill the big dreams that are in your heart or accomplish the great plans God has for your life. These seasons will not last forever, so learn everything you can from them while they do.

If you do not learn to endure, you will only know how to give up. Remember that developing your endurance today will help you run your race tomorrow. Sometimes, all you can do in a situation is to make it through, to bear it without buckling and without giving up. Even though endurance usually indicates survival instead of victory, you can not win without it. If you want to be a champion in life, the first thing you will have to do is endure. As you do, you will develop character, and that will lead to hope, which will turn around and enable you to endure again and again and again.

Whatever comes your way in life, set your mind to endure and to help others endure as well. Just as I learned to endure by watching my mother persevere through a long period of difficulty, someone is watching you — your son or daughter, a member of your extended family, people in your church or community. I believe that the best way to teach endurance is by example. You can tell a person all day long to be patient and to persevere, but that will not do much good. In the arena of endurance, the inspiration of an example will succeed where instructions fail. Let me encourage you to be an example of endurance when tests and trials present themselves to you and leave a legacy of perseverance for those who are not quite as far along as you are on the road of life. They are watching you, and you have the privilege of teaching them to endure, which will enable them to succeed.

Homework for the heart: What did you learn about endurance from your mother? What did she overcome in her lifetime that has inspired you to endure? What obstacles in your life are you presently overcoming? How can you inspire others through your example?

A mother's secret prayer: Heavenly Father, thank You for this day that You have given me, along with all the days past and the ones still to come. I pray that I will run with endurance and persevere through whatever trials or hardships the enemy of my soul might throw at me. I ask that my children learn to survive and thrive throughout the course of their life's journeys. Amen.

LESSON SIXTEEN
MAMAS TEACH US THAT EDUCATION IS EVERYWHERE

I have gone to school every day for as long as I can remember. No, I do not board a yellow bus with my lunch box and end up in a classroom, but I attend classes nevertheless. I look at life as a learning experience from start to finish, and I am determined to be a star pupil.

As I shared at the beginning of this book, my mother was a teacher, and I honestly cannot remember a time when I was not learning something. My brother, my sister, and I could all read and write before we started school because our mother was an educator. She taught us early on in our lives that education does not begin in a classroom and it is not limited to a school building. To her, the whole world was a classroom and everything in it was a teacher.

After roughly a half-century of being alive, I must say that I wholeheartedly agree with her. Now, please do not misunderstand me.

313

Formal education was a hallmark to my mother, and I realize with every passing day how much of an asset formal education is. But I want to be sure that we do not dismiss the fact that learning is more than textbooks and exams, quizzes and test scores. That's why I stress that our mothers are often our greatest teachers in this classroom called life.

They know as well as you and I do that there are many people who do have a formal education but who may not be well-educated. If they live in America, they begin in kindergarten or prekindergarten, they advance through the elementary grades, through the tumultuous junior high days and into high school. Those dedicated to the pursuit of higher education move on to college or university and then perhaps to the advanced levels of masters or doctoral work. These are the people who eventually have a string of letters behind their names; they often excel in their areas of expertise and make important contributions to society and to the world. Nonetheless, some of these people have much knowledge but haven't matriculated in the school of hard knocks to gain wisdom.

On the flip side, there are also people who have little or no formal education at all but who are incredibly wise. Some of them wanted more learning experiences than they had, but circumstances forced them to spend their time in other ways — perhaps getting a job because a parent had passed away or left or maybe was recovering from illness. Some people never were interested in learning or lost interest early on — and they discontinued their education at the first opportunity that presented itself. These people, too, often excel because their hardships made them strong and resourceful. They may not know how to find the square root of 437 or how to spell "Mediterranean," but they know how to get around in life, they know when someone is not telling the truth, they know what really matters, and they know how to enjoy living.

Whether a person has nine PhD's or never made it past the sixth grade, he or she needs to realize that education does not end when diplomas are presented or degrees are conferred. Otherwise, that person will stop learning and soon be completely unprepared to face the world. In my mind, to stop learning is to stop breathing because, truly, it keeps a person from being able to live and function in an ever-changing world.

Every day I live I learn something about life, about children, about others, about the world, about God. Learning about God will help us in every area of our lives. Oh, I am not talking about simply the technical theological information we gain about what He *does* (His acts), but I mean the more nebulous things we learn about who He is, and why and how He does what He does (His ways). As we commit our hearts and minds to understand the ways of God, we become eternal students. Learning to trust God's ways, cooperate with His plans, and participate in His purposes are not things we learn in a Greek or Hebrew class. No, those are part of spiritual learning and development, an education of the heart. These lessons and many others cannot be learned by listening to a lecture or reading a book; they come by inspiration. They are revelations that calm the soul and bring peace to the tormented mind.

As important as it is to be continually learning about God, it is also important to be students of humanity, because we will never stop interacting with other people. One of the many things that I learned as a youngster was to watch and learn about people. Created originally in the likeness of God, but marring that image, we now have a disfigured perception of ourselves and often even of our God. Though we are admittedly flawed, we are nonetheless interesting and I find watching people and their behavior an exhilarating pastime. For starters, the vast variety among our shapes and sizes fascinates me. I cannot even count the many shapes of ears and elbows, hands and hips, faces and feet I have seen over the years. I celebrate the differences between the tall and the short, the bald and the hirsute, the ones with delicate little noses and the ones with what we call a "schnoz," the lean and the pleasantly plump. Beyond that, I am also intrigued by the variety that exists in personalities, abilities, preferences, talents, ways of thinking, and approaches to life.

After nearly thirty years of ministry, I am still learning more and more about people; I suppose I will still be observing and enjoying the commonalities, complexities, and wonders of the human race thirty years from now. Some people astound me with their complete lack of schooling but their breathtaking gift of wisdom. Of course, if the truth be told, some amaze with their academic pedigrees and their utter deficit of common sense!

As I have already written, I have gone to school every day of my life. Some people have taught me what to do and some have taught me what not to do, but everybody has taught me something. My classrooms have included the rich and vibrant resources of the West Virginia mountainsides I roamed as a boy and the neighborhood where I grew up — where I first tried my hand at being a businessman by selling vegetables door to door. I also learned valuable lessons while I was employed as a ditchdigger, a paint salesman, and a foreman at a chemical plant. I never wanted the difficult coursework of unemployment, but it found me — so I decided to let it teach me its lessons.

As a minister, I have sat in the classroom of death row as I visited inmates whose last hope had been extinguished. I have spent time in the learning lab of a delivery room, several times, as I have watched new life take its very first breath — and, in other parts of the hospital, I have gained irreplaceable knowledge and wisdom as I have sat beside people as their days on earth drew to a close and they prepared to enter a realm where I have never been.

From Africa to Australia, Japan to Jamaica, New York to New Orleans, I have learned lessons that have enriched my life, informed my thinking, broadened my vision, expanded my capacities, and made me a stronger, more productive individual. I have

318

learned valuable lessons through winning and losing, through doing things well and through doing things wrong, through pain and through pleasure, through loss and through gain, through the ways of my children and through the words of my wife, through sunny days and starlit nights, through what I have said and what I have left unsaid, through triumph and through tragedy.

I have also gained quite an education from my mistakes. I know you have heard it said before, but it is true: we do learn from our mistakes. A mistake, by definition, is an innocent act birthed out of ignorance, bad information, or lack of experience. One touch of a tender toddler's finger on the eye of a burner will teach him quickly and permanently to stay away from the stove when it's hot. A series of tumbles will help an older child learn to balance on his bicycle after the training wheels have come off. A teenage girl attempting to find her own style learns how to dress and how to apply her makeup after her friends have cast disapproving glances. A young man only learns to wield a razor with skill after he suffers a few nicks on the chin. As we grow older, a variety of experiences help us learn that a pair of bifocals or a hearing aid or a walker could be a good idea. Mistakes can be tough teachers, but they are very effective.

I have never outgrown my love for learning. To this day, I am a voracious reader and a voracious listener. When I am in the presence of a person who is recognized as an expert in a particular field or profession, that person's words and insights are like a fresh stream of water on the dry sponge of my brain. I actively seek information I have never known before and am diligent to apply it to my life where appropriate. By the grace of God, I will be learning something until I breathe my last breath.

I want to encourage you, likewise, to approach your life as one grand learning experience, realizing that education is all around you. Take the time to ask more questions, gain more information, and probe more mysteries. Be eager to learn; be hungry to acquire and apply knowledge. Explore topics and issues and places and activities you know nothing about. Be curious, not complacent. Make sure your brain stays busy and that you do not miss the many learning opportunities that await you every day.

As you are continually learning, realize that you are also continually teaching. Your children, their friends, and other youngsters are watching you. You have the ability to teach them how to live their lives, face their fears, meet their challenges, leap the daily hurdles, and celebrate along the way. Do not be so hurried that you cannot take a moment to stop and explain to a child why you did what you did or said what you said, because when you do, you are providing an education. Help little minds grow by teaching them every chance you get. For example, when you are driving down the street with children in the car and you see a sunset, go beyond commenting on its beauty and tell the children that when the sun sets in your neighborhood, it rises on the other side of the world. Help them understand that people live in different countries, observe different customs, speak different languages, and are just waking up when others go to sleep. Or, when you see a butterfly, tell young children that the beautiful butterfly spent time in a cocoon and explain to them, on a very elementary level, that certain things take time.

As children grow, keep up with them. Begin to use movies, music, magazines, sports, the evening news, and other things they are interested in to provide education. For example, explain that three-pointers take practice or that a successful music career only comes with perseverance. Tailor all of your explanations to children and young people to their ages and stages of life, of course, but do not miss a chance to educate.

Truly, education is all around you. It never ends. Oh, of course, your formal schooling does have its milestones and points of completion (those are called "graduations"), but learning is constant and continual. Treat every place you go and every person you meet as a learning experience and treat every child you encounter as a teaching opportunity. For you, and for those who are watching you, education is everywhere.

Homework for the heart: What were your mother's hobbies and special interests? In what ways did she continue to learn throughout the course of her life? What do you wish you could spend some time learning more about? Make a wish list of places you'd like to visit, people you'd like to meet and question, and skills you'd like to learn. Choose one to pursue this week.

A mother's secret prayer: Dear God, I pray that I will remain curious and intrigued by this amazing world that You have placed me in. Help me to be a lifelong learner and to inspire my children to remain engaged with education that extends beyond the traditional classroom and formal degrees. Most of all, help us to remain lifelong learners of You and Your Word so that we might know You and love You more fully as we grow in wisdom. Amen.

SUBSTITUTE TEACHER
LEARNING FROM DELORES WINANS

Recently I was privileged to collect the comments of my friend CeCe Winans regarding her amazing mother, Delores "Mom" Winans. Shortly thereafter, I was summoned to Detroit to join the family in grieving and saying good-bye to Mom and Pop Winans's son Ronald, CeCe's brother, who died of a heart injury. During the incredible service, both a celebration of Ronald's life as well as a tribute to God's faithfulness even in our sorrow, many moving moments gripped my heart and stirred my soul. As BeBe and CeCe sang, I was amazed at this family's closeness and honest grieving over their loss. As I watched this large family united in their bittersweet loss — bitter because Ronald is gone from this earth and sweet because he is with our Lord in heaven, I turned my eyes to Mom and Pop, the anchors of this phenomenally talented and faithful family. Mom's eyes were plastered back with silent pain, with the fresh stabs of loss etched across her face. The soul of this mother was grieving. But even in this moment, God gave her grace that was also just as apparent in her carriage and presence. It was clear to me then that this strong, gentle matriarch would continue to sing the clear melody that had propelled her through her many decades of life and faith, the tune that allowed her children to sing harmony with her, the song that enabled her children to find their own chorus to carry them through life and its hardships. Her notes would remain clear and pure, full of joy and passion, sorrow and loss, but melodious throughout, a sweet praise offered up to God.

How does such a remarkable woman survive such a loss and continue to sing her life's melody, you may ask? As CeCe shares her mother with us, I think you will begin to understand something profound about what it means to persevere with abounding grace.

MY MOTHER, DELORES WINANS
CeCe Winans

"Great is Thy faithfulness, O God my Father." I suppose the hymn that opens with those timeless, familiar words is my mother's very favorite — and boy, can she sing it! In my mind, no voice on earth can equal the richness, the beauty, and the depth of heart with which my mother sings of the faithful God who has been her Father and her Friend for close to seventy years.

My mother, Delores Amelia Winans, known affectionately to so many around the world as Mom Winans, can sing of God's faithfulness with such passion because she has experienced it so often and so personally in so many situations, starting quite early in life. She was born in Michigan in the 1930s, and my mother's parents divorced when she was young, leaving my grandmother to raise her and her sister alone. Thankfully, my grandmother's mother was eager and able to help as well. Mom was raised by two good women, and I think all who know her would agree that she turned out terrific!

Mom has always been smart, she's always been diligent, she was even a good basketball player in her younger days. But more than those things, she has always been musical. Mom has been singing all of her life — throughout her childhood and into her teenage years. As an older teen, she joined a musical group called the Lemon Gospel

Chorus (because the man who started it was named Mr. Lemon). All the girls in the chorus had their sights set on a particular young man — at least that's what my father says! That young man, of course, is known today as Pop Winans, but back then he was the most desirable bachelor in the gospel group. His mother told him: "Delores will make the best wife for you." That settled it; their courtship began and when she was seventeen years old, my mother married my father. In November 2003, the two of them celebrated fifty years of happy, holy matrimony.

I do not write lightly about five decades of "happy, holy matrimony." My parents' lives have not been without challenge. Both of my parents were raised in broken homes. They did not have the example of a mother and a father to pattern their lives after. Instead, they looked to God's Word to find out how a husband and wife were to relate to each other and they modeled their marriage after the Bible. They have known plenty of hardship through the years, but they have stuck together. I like to say they just "kept staying and kept obeying."

In spite of the obstacles they have overcome — or maybe because of them — my parents' marriage has been graced with the joy of the Lord. Their relationship has indeed been a holy one, because my mother and father dedicated themselves to holiness when they first married. My father was raised in the holiness tradition and his grandfather was a holiness preacher. Mom was raised Baptist; her upbringing did not emphasize the principles of holiness as Pop's did. She loved the Lord, though, and when she married Pop, the two of them committed themselves to live holy lives, to have a holy marriage, and to raise their children in holiness and the fear of the Lord.

Raising their children to be holy must have been a challenge — simply because there were so many of us! There are seven boys, born all in a row, before my two sisters and I came along. On top of the sheer number of children in our family, Mom was sick for all nine months of every pregnancy. That means she was absolutely miserable for more than seven years of her life, just to bring us into the world! But somehow, by God's grace and by our parents' devotion to Him and to our family, all ten of us are loving and serving the Lord as adults. All of us are involved in music, most of us professionally. I suppose that is not hard to understand if you know that my great-grandfather once prayed and anointed his whole family, praying that they would all follow God and fulfill his call on their lives. I don't know if anything delights my parents as much as knowing that all of us are still doing just that, three generations later.

In addition to the emphasis on holiness in our home, we also had a strong focus on other Christian virtues — prayer, obedience to God's Word, church attendance, and loving other people. Every morning before we went to school, we all knelt together and Mom prayed with us. Then she kept praying as she sent us off! Not only were we raised in a house of prayer, our home was also filled with God's Word — we not only heard it spoken and were familiar with Bible verses or stories, we really knew the power of the truth of God's Word because we saw it at work in our parents' lives, and learned early on to apply it for ourselves. I always knew that as long as I obeyed God's Word, everything would turn out all right — and it always has.

On Sundays, there was never a question as to whether one of us would attend church. We had no choice; Mom *made* us go to church. We knew better than to ask to stay home or go somewhere else. Mom taught us to be Christians not only by praying, obeying God's Word, and being active in church, she also taught us to demonstrate our faith by loving other people. Mom is a real lover of people. She has an enormous, generous, loving heart and just being around her makes people feel loved and valued. She's always been that way. My siblings and I all agree that we always felt special to Mom. We never felt deprived by either of our parents, even though they had so many of us who needed and wanted their attention!

On top of her busy life inside our home, tending to each of us in special ways and raising us to be godly sons and daughters, Mom also held a job because having ten children created quite a financial need. I can remember many nights when we would drop Mom off at the Metropolitan Hospital in Detroit, where she was employed as a medical transcriptionist on the night shift. I always hated to see her go to work because I wanted her at home. I wasn't a possessive child; I simply loved being with Mom. In fact, I actually enjoyed going to the doctor because Mom always took me and I had her all to myself. After the doctor's visits, she always took me to a local restaurant (Saunders' in Detroit) for lunch and a cream puff hot fudge sundae (which is why I often tease her and say, "These hips are your fault!").

Along with her job at the hospital, Mom's dedication and elbow grease enabled her to meet all the practical challenges of a large family. As I mentioned, money was tight while we were growing up, but Mom was a good cook and our table was always a place of both natural and spiritual abundance. Mom was also quite a seamstress and she made many of our clothes. I have such fond memories of watching her sew late into the night. (I should have been asleep at those hours, but then again, so should she!) When we left home, we all looked nice because our mother not only had a spirit of excellence, but she sacrificed to make sure that the excellence of God was reflected in her family — first in our hearts, and then in the way we presented ourselves to the world.

Through all the hard work, through all the struggles and the joys, Mom never wavered, never compromised, never relaxed her godly standards. Lest you begin to think Mom's holiness would make her rigid or legalistic, let me say that holiness — the true holiness of the heart — made her happy, fun, full of life and laughter, so very loving, confident, radiant, and thoroughly at peace.

Now that I am grown, one of the things I most enjoy about my mom is watching her be a grandmother. My children — and I think this is true for all twenty-one of her grandchildren — have such enormous affection for her, and they love to be with her. They truly enjoy her company, but perhaps the greatest compliment of all is the fact that, according to them, she is *cool.* She treats them in much the same way she treated us as we were growing up — by simply encouraging and living her faith and her convictions in front of us.

I do not remember hearing many lectures from Mom. No, she chose to teach my siblings and me our life lessons primarily by example — and she taught me everything from how to persevere in prayer to how to make sure my husband is well-fed! She simply lived her life before us and allowed us to *see* dedication to the Lord, to *see* consistency, to *see* faith in action, to *see* unconditional love, to *see* generosity, to *see* humility, to *see* obedience to the Word.

I could never do too much for my mother or say too much about her. She is so gentle, yet so strong. She is my best girlfriend, a bright spot in my life every day that I live, a remarkable woman who is even more beautiful inside than out. Her praises will ring until the end of time and then, I'm sure, through the halls of heaven. Because God has given me such an excellent woman as my mother, I can add my own harmony to her sweet melody and join in: "Great is Thy faithfulness, O God my Father . . ."

have given me such an excellent woman as
my mother. I owe—and my own ambitions to
her, and my own wisdom and I am free—I can
fulfill my wishes and my dreams—

LESSON SEVENTEEN
MAMAS TEACH US TO SURVIVE
IN ORDER TO THRIVE

She was old by the time I met her. Her skin was leathery in texture, her hair still thick but white as snow upon her head. She seemed to me a very handsome woman in some slightly masculine way. The kind of life she led did not leave much room for primping or makeup. She was a woman beneath the trauma, but there had been no room in her life for the fine trinkets and frivolous shopping sprees that give a lady a makeover. No, hers was not Hollywood-style beauty. Her features were strong, her jaw was square, and her eyes piercing, almost as though somewhere down the line there was some Native American infusion in her DNA. She had that quiet calm, a spirit of wisdom that was almost like a black panther, stealthily eyeing the room with the keen ability of those who did not have education (the steady infusion of other people's opinions) to influence them and shape them.

Who was this fortress of a woman? She was not my mother, but my great-grandmother, Nancy Jakes, the mother of my paternal grandfather. She was a slave, and she taught me to survive.

We often tend to think of slavery as some event that occurred hundreds and hundreds of years ago, but its stench is still so close to us that I can faintly smell the odor of its atrocious toxic stink. I wonder how anyone survived it at all. But my great-grandmother, sitting in a room with a blanket cast across her aged knees and a generous dip of snuff under her tongue, was living proof that if you hold on and do not give up, you can survive the abuse, the night rapes, and the destruction that so many of her friends and family did not. Even at the age of about ten, when I went to visit her, I knew I was in the presence of a tower, an icon of fortitude.

I have often wondered about her childhood. *Nancy* was such a sweet name. It did not seem like a slave name. I imagined Nancy was little girl with a *big* smile and a frilly dress. But I knew that smiles and party dresses were not her life's experience. What did she do for the lack of toys? My own mother played with pecan shells and things that never seemed interesting to me. But this much older woman came from a time that was even more desolate than my mother's era. It was a dangerous time.

I have wondered, too, about her love life, her ideas and concepts, and what shaped her into the woman she was. I saw her daughter, my great-aunt Dinah, doting over her mother with the care and concern of a nurse and the discipline and tenacity of a veteran soldier. She too had inherited the grace her mother had — and the strength. But in her mother's eyes I saw secrets, some of which I am sure would never be told. You know, life is full of secrets; there are things we survive but do not discuss. There are victories that will never be celebrated, the narrow escapes from hell's kitchen that leave us deeply grateful but publicly silent.

Most of all, I have wondered where she found the strength to live through it all. I would love to have had the opportunity as a grown man to probe the depths of her heart and her mind, to have discovered exactly what is inside a person who triumphed over the evil that she conquered.

I well remember going to visit her, even though she died when I was in elementary school and when she was about one hundred years of age. Even though she was one of the oldest people I had ever seen, she was also one of the strongest, even in the frailty of her advanced years. Her house was simple. I do not suppose she ever experienced anything luxurious in her life — unless, of course, it belonged to someone else. Her place did not have air-conditioning, but that was not uncommon during those days. What caught my eye when I went to visit her was that her house always had more than the usual number of blankets. I knew that those blankets were intended to keep her warm in the wintertime, but I did not realize that they were essential because her house was not heated.

I can remember seeing her cook chicken on an old wood-burning stove. To my young mind, which had never known anything but freedom, having to haul wood and start a fire in the belly of a stove seemed like a lot of trouble. To my great-grandmother, though, I am sure it was a privilege. After all, it was her wood that she burned; it was her stove on which she cooked; the stove was in her house — and nobody told her when to do it or chided her if she did not do it exactly right. Because I had not suffered as she did, I viewed her blessing as a hardship.

Nancy Jakes seemed to know instinctively that it was important for her descendants, like me, to know and understand as much as possible about her life's experiences. We needed to know not only what our family members had endured, but what our people had endured. Because of her, I was able to sit with the kind of history book that others only read. Somehow, she managed to tell her stories with a note of triumph ringing through her every word. For that reason, I have a strong sense of cultural pride — not because my people were slaves, but *because my people survived.* I did not read or listen to something that had been recorded, but when my young fingers made contact with my great-grandmother's weathered skin, I held history in my hand. She did talk about her past, about what happened to her, and I had the excruciatingly painful privilege of hearing about it firsthand. That is something a person never forgets. It is an amazing awareness.

Whoever you are and whatever your heritage is, let me encourage you to study it and treasure it. Know the strengths and weaknesses of your people. Be acquainted with their triumphs and struggles, for those things belong to you. If at all possible, walk the land your ancestors worked and see the sights they saw. Spend time with the older members of your family and pull out of them the stories they heard from relatives you never knew. Be like a bucket drawing out fresh but ancient insights, facts, and anecdotes from the rich wells of their souls.

My children have the same sense of legacy and purpose that I do. I am thankful for that; it is good for them and it will be good for their children after them. They look at their ancestors not as slaves, but as survivors, and they know that survival is their birthright.

You see, my children have heard about Nancy Jakes for as long as they can remember. They know that I am named after her son. He was the first T. D. Jakes: I am the second and my son is the third. Nancy's son was an expert swimmer, and he often had to swim across a lake in order to get home from work. A group of angry white men put barbed wire into the lake one day, knowing that he would die a vicious, tortured death as he began his swim toward home that evening, which he did. Nancy Jakes, who was pregnant at the time, had to perform a mother's most agonizing duty — burying her child.

My great-grandmother's life was not easy. A person might think that being released from slavery would be a gigantic step toward a better life, but when we think about the barbed-wire trap set in the lake to kill her son, we realize that she climbed from one set of unbearable circumstances to another. She not only survived the horrors of slavery, but suffered even more at the cruel hand of racism after she was freed. I can still see her cold, black eyes. There were no signs of tears or sadness, just a steely resolution to keep on going, keep on surviving, until she too would leave this world behind.

I believe one of the mistakes we make when we become familiar with the past struggles and victories of our families is to stop when the stories end and to file them away in our minds as interesting tidbits of our personal history. What we must do instead is to take one step further and claim their trials and triumphs as our own, weaving them into the tapestries of our experience, drawing strength and courage from the spiritual, emotional, and mental DNA of those who have gone before us. Of course, we all have our unique challenges, our specific obstacles, our personal battles to fight — but as we confront these things, we can do so with the force of family valiance behind us and with the knowledge that their bravery runs in our blood.

The Bible teaches us in Hebrews 12:1 that

"since we are surrounded by so great a cloud of witnesses," that we can "lay aside every weight, and the sin which so easily ensnares us, and let us run with endurance the race that is set before us." Sometimes, when the going gets tough for me, I remember that I am surrounded by a great cloud of witnesses — and that Nancy Jakes is among them. I think these are the people who are cheering me on, sitting in the balconies of heaven, watching their loved ones on earth, clapping and whistling and calling our names with a rousing "You can do it!"

Personally, I have needed the foundation of survival that my ancestors built brick by brick in order to overcome and endure some tough situations. I have been blessed to achieve a measure of success and visibility in ministry and public service. As a result, I have weathered some storms and endured some controversy. I do not always have the opportunity to approve the comments that are made about me or the stories that are written. We live in a society that values free speech, so people can say anything they want to about me or about you. Our job is to live in such a way that we validate what is true and render the untruths utterly preposterous.

Success almost always leads to contro-versy. That's not easy for someone like me, who is still childlike at heart, who wants to believe the best about people, and who still wonders why everyone cannot just be nice. But I have been able to withstand the controversy because I come from a long line of survivors, women who used the pressure in their own lives to become better instead of bitter — and they all told me that I could survive the roughest of rides, the toughest of circumstances, and the harshest of criti-cism.

I want to make a point about my culture, the African American society: We are strongly matriarchal, and if there was a dif-ference to be made in a person's life, a mama made it. Many times it was your own mama, at times it was a grandmother or an aunt, but it was always somebody's mama. The women of our race have not only bred us and fed us, they have imparted strength and instilled courage. Over the years, I believe the greatest lesson they have taught us is the one I learned primarily from my great-grandmother, which is to survive the difficult days and the most grueling mo-ments of life, knowing that a brighter day will dawn — and that we will want to be around to enjoy it.

I learned from Nancy Jakes to survive and I want to pass that lesson along to you. Whatever you are going through, be determined to survive it. Tell your lungs to keep on breathing; tell your heart to keep on beating. No matter how difficult your days may be, determine to live them. Life will not always be so grueling, so just keep going. Survive the dark days because eventually morning will come. All you have to do is keep on going until it does.

Homework for the heart: What are some of the life events that your mother survived? What did she pass along to you from these encounters with hardship? Why is it so important to know where you came from in order to survive and move forward through your own challenges?

A mother's secret prayer: Most gracious God, I thank You for the many ways You have helped me survive hardships by learning from those who survived and thrived before me. Help me to pass such a spirit of survival on to my children, that they may know their true substance and thrive. Amen.

LESSON EIGHTEEN
MAMAS TEACH US TO BE WISE

Newborn babies do not come with instructions. A woman does not know everything about being a mother the minute she gives birth. She does have God-given instincts, and she does have intuition (which we'll discuss in more detail momentarily), but she does not have all the answers. As her children grow, she can and should consult other mothers whose experience with children excels her own and read books about parenting. She should learn how to changes diapers properly, how to bathe an infant, and what to do with a runny nose, how to get strained peas out of superfine hair, and how to tell the difference between a situation that warrants a call to the doctor and one that does not.

But mothering is far more than mechanics. The mechanics are necessary because, after all, babies need to be bathed. But beyond the logistical skills a mother must

345

master and the common sense she must employ, she needs something else. Yes, skills will enable her to take care of children physically, but in order to tend their hearts, she must have wisdom.

Often a woman who discovers she is pregnant feels intimidated. She cries when no one is looking and secretly fears she will not be a good mother. But, you know, good mothers, like children, are often developed over time. There is more to mothering than the initial skills of burping a baby and wrapping her or him up in a sleeper at night. The challenges mount as the years go by. The early years of mothering might in fact be the easiest part. I know that may be scary to young mothers who are often exasperated by the challenges of getting the baby in the car seat, the breast milk expressed into the travel container, and the footies packed for the vacation. But in reality that is nothing compared to the years of puberty, adolescence, dating, and the "guess who's coming to dinner" phase!

But the good news is that "as your days, so shall your strength be" (Deuteronomy 33:25), which simply means that as the challenges mount, so will the wisdom. God is so wise that He releases wisdom like a time-release medicine capsule. You may not have it all at once. But when it is time, the wisdom you need will be there for you. If you do not sense it, seek it. It will come.

I will address this matter of asking God for wisdom in greater detail later in this chapter, but for now let me say that I find that if you ask God for wisdom, He has a way of giving you answers to tough questions — such as, "Mama, is Santa Claus real?" Such inquiries may be easier to answer than other questions about love, sexuality, depression, and other issues that will arise over the years. You, my dear, have to be not only a source of answers for your children, but a secret-keeper as well. Your heart has to be a vault filled with their treasures and sometimes even their trash. But when it becomes overwhelming, and it will, take it to the Lord and leave it there. He will give you beauty for ashes and strength for the challenge. He will renew you and encourage you, and every experience will increase your wisdom. By the time your hair is gray, your heart should be filled with golden pearls of wisdom!

Sometimes, when we hear the word "wisdom," we think of a gift that is reserved for a select few or of something that comes only with age and gray hair. But wisdom is for everyone, and we all need it. God delights to give to all who ask, and He knows that mothers often need an extra dose because of the unique challenges they face!

A wise mother will know how to answer tricky questions, mediate conflict between siblings, discipline without destroying a child's spirit, bring healing to hurt feelings, inspire her children to do the right thing, navigate the gray areas of life, execute justice in her home, resist favoritism, and impart courage. She will know when to hold them tightly and when to insist that they flap their own wings, when to practice tough love and when to be tender, when to enforce her authority and when to be merciful. Perhaps best of all, a wise woman will produce people who will also be wise someday.

The Old Testament prophet Jeremiah knew the value of wise women. God had appointed him to prophesy bad news to the kingdom of Judah, warning them of impending doom as a result of their sin. In the beautiful old King James version of the Bible, we read his words:

Thus saith the LORD of hosts, Consider ye, and call for the mourning women, that they may come; and send for cunning women, that they may come: And let them make haste, and take up a wailing for us, that our eyes may run down with tears, and our eyelids gush out with waters. For a voice of wailing is heard out of Zion, How are we spoiled! We are greatly confounded, because we have forsaken the land, because our dwellings have cast us out. (Jeremiah 9:17–19, KJV)

I want you to notice that God Himself calls for "the mourning women" and for "the cunning women." Do you know that in Hebrew, the word for "cunning" means "wise and skillful" in English? In a time of crisis, God sent for the wise and skillful women. In times of crisis today, which seem to be more and more frequent, and in our everyday lives, we desperately need wisdom.

We gain wisdom by paying attention when we are in the presence of wise people who will share what they have learned; we develop it as we do some things right — but more things wrong — in life; we can get it from reading certain books. But most of all we receive it as a gift from God. James 1:5–6 tells us how: "If any of you lacks wisdom, let him ask of God, who gives to all liberally and without reproach, and it will be given to him. But let him ask in faith, with no doubting, for he who doubts is like a wave of the sea driven and tossed by the wind." If you have ever wondered what the secret to wisdom might be, you now have your answer: ask. Yes, it is that simple. Just ask God to give you wisdom, and you will get it. His Word promises that He will give it liberally as long as you ask with faith in your heart. He wants a world full of wise women, and He will make you one if you will put in your request and refuse to doubt His desire or ability to grant it.

While God will give you wisdom when you ask, He will not just deposit it in you while you sleep. No, you will have to do your part to search for it, as you would with any treasure — and you start by looking in God's Word. I believe that a woman's greatest source of wisdom is the Bible. Earlier in this book, I mentioned King Solomon, who was often called "the wisest man who ever lived." The Old Testament contains several of Solomon's writings, many of which help us understand what wisdom is, where it comes from, and how it benefits us. Here are just a few of the glittering truths adorning the crown of wisdom from this wisest of men.

    1. *Wisdom makes people happy.* "Happy is the man who finds wisdom, and the man

who gains understanding" (Proverbs 3:13).

2. *Wisdom is better than all the money in the world and more precious than jewels.* "For her proceeds are better than the profits of silver, and her gain than fine gold. She is more precious than rubies" (Proverbs 3:14–15). "How much better to get wisdom than gold! And to get understanding is to be chosen rather than silver" (Proverbs 16:16).

3. *Wisdom is incomparably better than anything a person could ever want.* "All the things you may desire cannot compare with her" (Proverbs 3:15 and 8:11).

4. *Wisdom brings long life, riches, and honor.* "Length of days is in her right hand, in her left hand riches and honor" (Proverbs 3:16).

5. *Wisdom brings pleasantness and peace.* "Her ways are ways of pleasantness, and all her paths are peace" (Proverbs 3:17).

6. *Wisdom is a source of nourishment for the soul and those who are wise are also happy.* "She is a tree of life to those who take hold of her, and happy are all who retain her" (Proverbs 3:18).

7. *Wisdom is the most important of all earthly pursuits.* "Wisdom is the principal

thing; therefore get wisdom" (Proverbs 4:7).

8. *Wisdom starts with fearing God, which does not mean being afraid of Him, but having a deep, reverent respect for Him.* "The fear of the LORD is the beginning of wisdom, And the knowledge of the Holy One is understanding" (Proverbs 9:10). "The fear of the LORD is the instruction of wisdom, and before honor is humility" (Proverbs 15:33).

9. *Wisdom helps people establish and build strong, godly homes and families.* "Through wisdom a house is built, and by understanding it is established" (Proverbs 24:3). "The wise woman builds her house, but the foolish pulls it down with her hands" (Proverbs 14:1).

10. *Wisdom is always preferable to foolishness.* "Then I saw that wisdom excels folly as light excels darkness" (Ecclesiastes 2:13).

11. *Wisdom will protect you.* "For wisdom is a defense as money is a defense, but the excellence of knowledge is that wisdom gives life to those who have it" (Ecclesiastes 7:12).

12. *Wisdom leads to success.* "If the ax is dull, and one does not sharpen the edge,

then he must use more strength; but wisdom brings success" (Ecclesiastes 10:10).

I believe that a woman's second greatest source of wisdom, after the Bible, is her God-given intuition. Men laugh, at times, about women's intuition, but do not be deceived: men know that it exists and they know how often a woman is right because of it. Men do not really understand it, but they know they should trust it, even when they do not appear to be taking it seriously. A wise man knows that a woman's intuition is one of his best secret weapons.

Intuition is amazing; it is the voice of a woman's heart. Intuition tells a mother when her child has been into the cookie jar, even when she was nowhere near the kitchen. It alerts her when her son or daughter is not telling the truth. It enables her to know when her teenage daughter's boyfriend is up to no good. In fact, seemingly, intuition allows a mother to know everything her children have done wrong. But it also gives her a strong sense of what her children do right, what they are good at, how they may excel in the future, what gifts and abilities she needs to make sure are developed in their lives. It is not only an internal tattle-tale; it is also a forecaster of destiny.

If you are a mother, I want to encourage you to pay attention to your intuition. Listen to the voice inside of you, for it will guide you. Trust what your heart tells you. It will direct you in matters pertaining to your own life and to the lives of your children.

You may take exception to my suggestion here. You may be thinking of all the times you "followed your heart" and ended up abandoned or abused. You may be remembering moments when your heart misled you. I need to tell you that I have met many women over the years whose hearts have been so battered and broken that they speak nothing but anger, jealousy, bitterness, or resentment. A heart in that condition will indeed lead a woman astray.

A woman whose heart has been devastated simply needs the healing touch of God in her life. If you have been wounded in any way, ask God to heal your hurts and make your heart whole again. This may not happen overnight; it may take a while, because deep works often do. But let me encourage you to let the healing begin. Ask Him to do such a healing, cleansing, restoring work that you will be able to trust what your heart says to you. Ask Him to help you recognize the voices of bitterness or rejection or anger. One of the gifts God gives His children through the Holy Spirit is the ability to discern between the godly and the ungodly, between the true and the false. He wants every voice within you silenced except His own — and I believe that is what you want too, because His is the only voice you can trust.

Jesus addresses this issue in John 7:38 when He says: " 'He who believes in Me, as the Scripture has said, out of his heart will flow rivers of living water.' But this He spoke concerning the Spirit, whom those believing in Him would receive; for the Holy Spirit was not yet given, because Jesus was not yet glorified." If you are a believer in Jesus Christ, then you can trust that there are rivers of living water in your heart. That means that life-giving, life-changing truth is flowing within you by the power of the Holy Spirit.

Rivers of living water will flush out every other inner voice that tries to get your attention. Do not let the junk of unforgiveness, jealousy, resentment, and other painful, destructive emotions pollute the water within you. Keep that fresh, clean, living stream flowing freely and deeply by worshipping God, spending time in His presence, reminding yourself of His love, believing His Word, praying and fellowshipping with other believers. Do not let your stream become stagnant, for just as water that does not move is a breeding ground for disease in the natural world, so a stagnant heart will also be susceptible to things that are unhealthy.

Pure intuition in an unpolluted heart makes a woman extremely wise indeed, for it is graced with the wisdom of God. Let me encourage you to do everything you need to do to keep a clean heart before Him. If you have been wounded in such a way that your heart is contaminated, ask God to heal you and to provide you with any resources, people, or services you may need in order to experience true and lasting healing. Then, rivers of living water will flow out of you and you will be able to trust what your heart says and receive it as the leadership of the Holy Spirit. The more you do that, the wiser you will be. And when God sends for a wise woman, He will be calling your name.

Homework for the heart: What are some of the ways your mother revealed her wisdom? When did she display her intuition in action? What did she teach you about wisdom? How are you seeking to grow wiser in your own life? If your mother is still living, and of a sound mind, call her this week and seek her advice on a matter you are currently considering.

A mother's secret prayer: Dear Lord, You are all-knowing and the source of all wisdom. I ask that I might learn from Your Word and harness my feminine intuition in order to be a truly wise woman. Thank You for providing insight and clarity, discernment and decisiveness as I live each day. I pray that my children will benefit from such wisdom and that they will also seek You as the source of all knowledge. Amen.

LESSON NINETEEN
MAMAS TEACH US TO DIE WITH THE DOORS CLOSED

As I have already written in this book, we all want to finish well. When the curtain falls on our lives, we want to feel good about our days on earth — to believe that we made a difference in someone's life, to believe that the world was a better place simply because we were in it. Most of us intend to die with our affairs in order, with our families provided for, with our bills paid, and with our last will and testament in order. Some people burn their journals or diaries when they know that death is near; others want to leave a written record of their lives for their loved ones to read. Some people want to be buried, some want to lie in a mausoleum, others want to be cremated and have their ashes scattered over the open sea, carried by the wind to places they themselves never got to see.

However people choose to think about the end of their lives, we all have one thing in common. We know that death is final. We are well aware that our last arrangements are indeed final, that there is no going back to redo what we wish had been different.

We never know when death will come. Sometimes it surprises us by taking people who seem far too young for a casket. Sometimes it breaks our hearts by waiting so long that a person's suffering becomes far more agonizing than their home going. Sometimes we see it coming, but that does not make us ready for it.

One thing is absolutely certain: you will die someday. When you do, I pray that you will enter into the glorious eternity that God has prepared for you and that you will walk the streets of heaven with joy and peace beyond anything you have ever known on earth. But before any of us arrives at that blessed destination, we need to make sure that we live well while we have breath and that we die well when the time comes. I learned a critical lesson when my mother slipped from this world into the next, a lesson I believe will greatly benefit you and those who love you. I call it "dying with the doors closed."

After we have lost someone we love, after the eulogies have been given and the flowers have been lovingly tossed on the grave, we must all begin to live again. As the numbness of death wears off, we often start thinking such thoughts as these: *I wish I had asked him . . . , I wish I had told her . . . , I wish I knew what he thought about . . . , I wish I had found out . . .* Our grief becomes tainted with wishes and regrets.

I want you to know that it does not have to be this way. You may have lingering questions or concerns inside yourself and may be living with the knowledge that you will never obtain the answers you long for, but you can avoid having that happen again both to you and to those who will someday mourn you.

As a pastor, I have been privileged to witness countless entrances to eternity. My ears have heard the haunting of the "death rattle" and the peaceful, gentle, gradual sigh of a final exhale. My eyes have seen numerous chests rise and fall, and rise and fall, and then stop in stillness. My heart has wept with those who were weeping, grieved with those who were grieving, and stood quietly beside those who knew that death was preferable to earthly life for some people. I have rejoiced with those who had a revelation of heaven and who through their tears could still see clearly enough to look forward to a great and happy reunion someday on "the other side."

On many occasions after a death, I have observed that the survivors' biggest challenges come from unanswered questions and unresolved issues. Those things often produce more torment, create more confusion, and leave a larger hole in a living person's heart than the actual departure of a family member or a friend.

In my years as a minister, I have attended and conducted many funerals, and time after time I have witnessed loved ones standing near a casket screaming for forgiveness or weeping at a mausoleum trying to explain why they did not come to this or that, or why they did not express something. I have seen people kissing the dead, waiting until it was too late to express forgiveness or admit they were wrong about something. These are the sad memories of lost opportunities — most of these opportunities lost because of pride, which can rob a person of a great relationship and a true sense of peace.

You would never imagine how many people find themselves trying to settle old accounts with the dead. Much like a vacant house whose door has been left gaping open, the cold winds rush through the house unchecked. Like a house, the human soul has doors, and unanswered questions leave those doors standing painfully open: "Who was my father?" "Why didn't you raise me?" "What happened between you and my father?" Questions like these are the doorstops that leave the heart wide open and the soul in agony that is worse than grief itself. Sadly, these doors do not close easily after a person is gone.

All kinds of creatures can enter a house when a door is left open. The same is true with our minds. Unanswered questions invite all kinds of thoughts. They can lead to misunderstanding and to inappropriate guilt. So let me encourage you to resolve the issues that need to be resolved with the people who care about you. Answer even the tough ones, *especially* the tough ones. Some of those questions will be left over from days long gone and some will be immediate. I can assure you that if you suffer a prolonged illness and if you require medical attention for any length of time, the people responsible for your medical affairs will want to know whether you were happy with the care they arranged for you. If you are not happy, let them know while you are able to. People who love you need to know that you think they did their very best for you. That knowledge will comfort them when you are gone. If your children are the ones caring for you, then no matter how old they are, they still need to know that you are proud of them and that you believe they made good decisions.

Occasionally, people ask me what I think my greatest accomplishment is. I will tell you: The thing I am most proud of in life is that I took care of my mother until she breathed her last breath. I had the distinct privilege of being able to love someone back, to return to her the depth and the quality of love she gave to me. That has been the greatest honor of my life. Truly, one of my great privileges in life was to get to say "thank you" to her in a variety of ways as I cared for her during her illness. God paid her back. She did not die alone; she slipped out of my arms and into the arms of God, like the most noble of queens stepping out to meet her King.

As she was dying, she said to me one day, "You know what? If my mother had gotten the care you give me, she'd still be living." I said to her, "Mother, if your mother were still living she would be well over a hundred years old." She looked at me with the same gaze she used when teaching students a new idea or principle that was hard to grasp. And I realized that her mother's age was not the point. Her comment was her way of telling me how much she appreciated my care for her in the final days, weeks, and years of her life. One thing my mother knew was that her children loved her. Each of us gave her love and attention in our own way to make her know how grateful we were to her. But she also gave us the gift of accepting that love and appreciating us. She left no room for guilt. Oh yes, we had massive grief when she passed, but no guilt. Mother had spoken — and she always had the last word!

I appreciate so very much that my mother closed that door and every other one before she died. She answered every question I had. She was still closing doors on the way out of her earthly house. I asked the questions I wanted answered at that time, and I asked the questions I knew I would want answered eventually, and she, with her mother's intuition, addressed issues she knew would be important to me. That way, as I have already written, I had grief, but I did not have guilt, after she was gone.

I thought that death would take her away from me, but it has actually made her seem closer. I can be anywhere and hear her voice. People we love never really leave us; we just cannot see them anymore. I think that is what "love is stronger than death" means. Death does not stand a chance against love. That's why Jesus Christ got up from the grave.

And so the lesson I would pass along to you about dying with the doors closed is: Parents, communicate with your children. Children (of any age), communicate with your parents. Whoever you are and whatever your role in the lives of other people, communicate with those you love. If you love someone, tell them. If you judged them too severely or if you have been too religious and not close with someone, apologize. Church people often allow their convictions to become so strong that they fail to reach out to their own children or parents, fighting instead over doctrine or religious conjecture. Mama taught me a good lesson: open your mouth and speak healing and love.

It is better to close the doors while your hands are warm. You would be surprised what an apology or a compliment, a kiss or a confession, can do. A word of appreciation can chase away a world of condemnation. Not one of us would walk out of someone's home and leave the door standing wide open, so why would we risk dying without setting the house in order and closing all the doors? Refuse to die with the doors open. Answer the questions because eventually, all your loved ones will have is what you have told them. That is all I have. But do you know what? That is all I need. Give the gift that keeps on giving. Say what needs to be said while those who need to hear it can do so.

Homework for the heart: Based on whether your mother is still living, reflect for a moment on either her passing from this life or her attitude toward passing when her time comes. What have you learned from her about what it means to live fully until your time here has ended? If your mother is still living, what do you need to tell her before she goes? If she has already passed, what do you wish you had told her?

A mother's secret prayer: Heavenly Father, thank You for this life that You have given me. I pray that I would continue to live fully and vibrantly all the remaining days that You provide. And when it comes time to go home to You, I pray that I would pass from this life with dignity and the distinction of knowing that I served You as faithfully as I could. I ask that my children would celebrate my homecoming and use their remaining time wisely as they seek to live with integrity in glorifying You. Amen.

SUBSTITUTE TEACHER
LEARNING FROM VADA HAGEE

My mother traveled outside our country only twice in her lifetime. The last time was when she was suffering from the disorienting throes of Alzheimer's disease and wanted to go to the beach and put her feet in the sand once more, as she did as a kid along the Carolina coast. I was privileged to take her to the Bahamas, where she marveled at the beautiful, opaque blue-green waters and the diamond crystal sand of their lovely beaches.

The other occasion was a trip to Germany she had taken years before. Knowing the lifelong curiosity that my mother expressed, you will not be surprised to learn that she loved visiting this fascinating culture and its people. From the Rhineland to Bavaria, my mother feasted on the sights and sounds of this timeless center of European history. Of all the many experiences she enjoyed, Mama loved meeting the people there more than anything. She found them to be stern and strong as well as kind and gracious, passionate people often keeping their excitement for life beneath a calm exterior.

I think of that trip now because my mother and I discussed the way that ethnic heritage and culture make a tremendous difference in the way that parents raise their children. And that certainly emerges in our final portrait of an influential mother, Mrs. Vada Hagee. With his robust stature and fiery nature, John Hagee embodies his mother's passion and commitment to the faith like no one else. You can almost hear the little German woman (with the Texas accent!) speaking through him, in the tenacity and intensity of his speech and gifted preaching. Yes, our heritage and cultural roots manifest themselves in our upbringing, providing a lifeline between the sacrifices and triumphs of the past generations and the exciting possibilities waiting in future offspring. I'm delighted to have my friend John Hagee provide a powerful example of this generational bridge through his description of his loving mother.

MY MOTHER, VADA SWICK HAGEE
John Hagee

Truly, heaven touched earth on May 29, 1913, when my mother was born to Martha and Charles Albert Swick of Alice, Texas. I wonder if her father, a rancher, and her mother, a registered nurse, realized the importance of that day or knew what a gift they had given the world as they held their little daughter. I wonder if they ever dreamed that God's healing power would one day flow through her tiny hands. Did they know how much time her chubby little knees would spend on the floor in earnest, heartfelt prayer? Could they have ever imagined that their newborn baby's cries would one day become the tears of God as she wept over those who do not know Him?

Her father did not live to see his beautiful daughter become the remarkable woman she is today. Several years after Mother was born, her family moved to Goose Creek, Texas (now known as Baytown), where her father applied for a job at Wright's Shipyard. During his physical examination, the doctor discovered that he had a hernia that had to be repaired before he could begin work.

Charles Albert Swick died from the consequences of that simple surgery, leaving my mother, then seven years old, with her mother and six children to survive without him. My grandmother had to go to work, and because there were no hospitals in Baytown, she went to the homes of people who were sick and stayed with them Monday through Friday. Her necessary absences required her to turn the care and supervision of the home over to my mother. With such tremendous responsibilities at such an early age, my mother never had the luxury of being a child. From her youth, my mother has always been the person in charge!

Mom left home for Bible college when she was eighteen with a burning passion to serve the Lord. She worked her way through Bible college, obtaining her bachelor's degree in theology from the Raymond T. Richie School of Theology in Houston. She started preaching at the age of twenty and was soon speaking across the length and breadth of America in the largest churches and auditoriums available at that time. Her potential pulpit ministry had no limits. In fact, I am sure that if I could erase fifty years from her life and put her on national television today, she would melt the screen!

Mother is a natural-born orator, and she can still paint verbal portraits that are alive and electric. She can describe Jesus and His twelve disciples crossing the Sea of Galilee so vividly you can feel the water splash on your face. In her younger years, she taught prophetic themes, using charts she drew — charts with such shocking clarity that you were certain the Antichrist was in the lobby of the church.

However, Mother did not just preach the Word of God; she intimately believed it and reaped its good fruit in her own life and in the life of our family. Her greatest challenge in my childhood began the day she received a phone call from the middle school my brother attended, saying, "Your son has passed out in class. Would you please come to the school immediately?"

My family had always enjoyed excellent health, so the fact that my brother had passed out in school was shocking news that turned to tragedy when the doctor said, "Your son has grand mal epilepsy in its worst form." Then, the doctor told my mother not to allow my older brother to climb a tree, ride a bicycle, or do anything that would endanger his life when he passed out several times a day with these hideous seizures.

At that time, in the 1940s, medical science had very few solutions for grand mal epilepsy. My mother brought my brother home from the doctor's office in Houston and boldly proclaimed to our family, "God will heal Bill. I will fast and pray every supper meal until he is completely and perfectly healed." For three years, my mother fasted and prayed the supper meal for my brother, no exceptions. On Thanksgiving, Christmas, anniversaries, and special events, Mother's chair was empty because she was in her bedroom speaking to the Great Physician about the health of her oldest son.

God, in His eternal faithfulness, healed my brother. He is seventy years old today and in great health because our mother knew the power of prayer and was relentless in her persistence before the throne of God. Mother always told me that all Heaven had to offer to any man was given only to those who pray. Her statement was, "Some prayer, some power. More prayer, more power. Much prayer, much power."

My mother and father were pastors for fifty years in the General Council of the Assemblies of God, so our lives were lived in and around the church. Prayer, God's Word, and spiritual things were part of the fabric of our daily activities. One special memory I have of Mother is the day I came home from football practice at Reagan High School in Houston. She was standing at the sink, washing dishes. Her Bible was open to the book of James in the window, as she made a habit of reading and memorizing Scripture when she washed the dishes.

When I walked in the back door, I saw tears streaming down my mother's face. I was not saved at the time, but I knew my mother was spiritually focused on a target. I just hoped her target was not me! As I sat down at the table, Mom turned to me and said, "John, the little boy who just moved next door has epilepsy. I'm going to go over to his house and pray for him. God is going to heal him today."

As for me, I did not want to project the image of being "fanatical" to our new neighbors. I expressed my concern to my mother, who did not bother to waste her time responding. Instead, she put down her dish towel, stormed out the door, and marched across the alley on a mission from God. My face was red in anticipation of what was about to happen. When Mother starts praying, Heaven gets in high gear. She is a purebred Pentecostal with the vocal thunder of a firetruck racing to a five-alarm fire.

That day was no exception. Mom introduced herself to the lady next door and asked if she could pray for her son. Fortunately for them, they let her in. She told them God had healed her son of epilepsy, and she was certain God would heal their son too. I could hear Mother praying from our kitchen table, where I was trying to eat supper.

The neighbors moved the next week. I thought it was to escape the religious fanatics across the alley, but when we saw them one year later in the supermarket, the woman came running up to my mother, waving her arms and shouting, "From the day you prayed for my son, he has not had another seizure! We are so thankful for your coming to our home and praying for our son."

Not only did Mother pray with intensity and power, she also taught us to pray specifically and intensely. She prayed with her sons every night, but we had an extended time of prayer on Saturday nights. Mother taught us, "Ask God so specifically for what you want that when you get it, you will know that only God could have sent it." I have practiced the power of this kind of specific prayer ever since, and learning to pray in such a way is one of the greatest lessons my mother ever taught me.

On Saturday nights, my mother would kneel beside me (and each of my brothers in turn) and pray this prayer: "Lord, if in Your providence You see that my son John would grow up and live a godless life and bring shame to Your name, I pray that You would take him as a child." Believe me, when you hear that prayer coming out of your mother's mouth, it makes an impression on you. To this day, I still have the awesome reverence for God that Mother burned into my brain as a child.

Saturday nights also held another regular activity at our house — preparing our clothes for church on Sunday. In fact, as children, we had to put out our clothes, our shoes, our Bibles, and everything we needed for Sunday morning. I am not talking about simply choosing what to wear; I mean that we *really* had to get our clothes ready. My mother taught me to wash and iron my clothes when I was only six years old. It didn't take me long to figure out that ironing was not fun. I tried to dodge the unpleasant task by doing it sloppily, thinking that good ol' Mom would step in and do it for me. I was wrong. Mother demanded excellence, and would say often, "If you don't do it right the first time, when are you going to have the time to do it over?" So she let me do my ironing — over and over and over — until my shirt or pants were fit to wear in public, so that I would learn to do it right. Today, I can iron as well as any woman alive, and if you were to call me on any given Saturday night of my life, you would find me at the ironing board!

There are not enough pages left in this book to articulate all the ways my mother has made a difference in my life or all of her best qualities because she truly is a portrait of the Proverbs 31 woman of God. If I had to select just one of her outstanding attributes, though, it would be her role as an absolute disciplinarian, with rules etched in granite. She was never intimidated or manipulated by what other parents allowed their children to do or not to do. The "herd instinct" certainly never affected the Hagee household!

If my mother told you she would spank you with a switch for disobedience, you could bank on it. Appealing for a stay of execution was a complete waste of time! The only appellate court in our house was my father, and lunch with a hungry lion was teatime compared to his discipline. But when Mom disciplined us, she never did so in anger. She disciplined as methodically as if she were drinking a glass of water. In her mind, if you broke the rules and she allowed you to "get by" with it, she felt she was an accomplice to evil and was causing the spirit of rebellion to prosper in the lives of her four sons. As I'm sure you can tell by now, she would not stand for that!

Her discipline never left our lives, and I am certain that there have been times in my life when I would have considered giving up without the persistent discipline she instilled in me as a very young boy. As far back as I can remember, quitting a project once we started it was unthinkable. My mother could have been a drill sergeant, and apparently, my older brother thought so too after he joined the army at the age of eighteen. I will never forget his first letter home, which read, "Dear Mom and Dad, I love the Army. There's only one difference between home and the Army — you get paid here. I don't think I'll ever leave." He did leave, but not until thirty years later, and he enjoyed every day of his service.

But our home was not all rules and regulations; we also had fun. In my early years, television was not yet an American disease and we all checked out books from the mobile library van that came to our school. My mother was a passionate reader and she taught me to read early and to read often. In addition to reading, one of our family's favorite activities was to sing and play music. In the evenings, after we washed the supper dishes, Mother would go to the piano, Dad would get his guitar, my brother Bill would tune his stand-up bass violin, and I would get my saxophone. Together we would sing and play the songs of the church until the shingles on the roof would rattle with joy. We had such good times when we made music together. But I have to tell you, I got off to a rocky start when it came to making music with my mother.

When I was five years old, my mother made an announcement to me: "You are going to sing a solo at church this Sunday." I told her that I did not want to sing in front of so many people. It was a small church of about 250 people, but to a five-year-old singing his first solo, 250 is a multitude.

I might as well have responded to my mother that day by saying, "I'm thrilled," because my lack of desire did not cause her to let me off the hook. Instead, she promptly introduced me to the song "The One Lost Sheep." She sat down at the piano, put a switch on the music rack (I knew what that meant!), and said, "When you learn this you can go play football." I learned the song in record time.

The next Sunday, I began singing "The One Lost Sheep" standing behind the pulpit with my nose against the wood. I was terrified to peek out across the congregation and look all those people in the face. Mother was not impressed. She walked up onto the platform, led me out from behind the pulpit, and informed everyone that we would be starting over.

One day she brought home a Hawaiian guitar and said, "I want you to learn to play this." I didn't even know what it was. It had a manual showing me how to hook up the guitar to the amplifier. I read the instruction book and managed to learn the musical scale. Within six weeks it clicked, and I started playing the guitar in church. There was never the idea, once Mother said, "Do it," that it would not happen. I truly thank God for helping me — or I would still be playing that guitar!

At age seventeen I left home for Bible college. Ever since the day I left my parents' home, I have tried to call my mother on the phone at least once a week to tell her I love her and to give her a spiritual report of what is happening in the ministry.

Just two months after I left home, I preached my first sermon the first Sunday of March 1958. Two weeks later, I preached that same sermon in an Assemblies of God church in Dallas, during the youth service.

The pastor of the church was present and asked me if I would preach the same sermon to the general congregation that night. I agreed. There were many salvations that night, and the pastor asked the congregation, "How many of you would like to start a revival with Brother Hagee tomorrow night?" Every hand in the congregation shot up.

My heart stopped! I only had one sermon, and I had just preached it twice in the same church on the same night. I expressed my concerns to the pastor, who slapped me on the back and said, "Son, you were born to preach. Just show up, and Jesus will do the rest."

I'll admit my faith was not nearly as strong as the pastor's. I drove to the dormitory and called Mother. I told her what had happened, and she said, "It's midnight. Go to bed and get up at six in the morning. Go to the prayer room and ask God to give you a divine thought for that congregation. When you get that thought, call me."

Mother had taught homiletics in Bible college. The next morning I got the thought, called Mother, and she outlined a masterpiece, which I quickly wrote on paper and took to Dallas that night. Heaven came down! It really was a tremendous service, so

I continued to ask God for divine thoughts and relay them to my mother, who outlined my sermons — for fourteen days! The church was packed to the walls, despite a snowstorm. After two weeks, the pastor got up and announced that we would continue the revival for a third week. I thought I would die! You guessed it: I called Mother.

Thanks to her devoted mother's heart and her brilliant brain, we managed another seven sermons. When services began the last Sunday night, I said to the pastor, "I'm done." To this day, when I make my weekly phone calls to Mother, she will say, "I heard you say something in your sermon that I want you to clarify. Get your Bible, and let's talk."

In mid 2004, I called to tell Mother that I had agreed to go to Nigeria later that year and that I would be preaching the Gospel to at least two million people who would gather at the campground of the Church of the Redeemed. She wept until she could not speak. Nothing moves my mother more than the conversion of a single soul — and the thought that thousands may be converted in one night was more than she could contain. She said, "I would love to go. Please take pictures so I can see what two million people look like listening to the

Gospel of Jesus Christ." No wonder my Mother's favorite Bible verse and theme of her life is Proverbs 11:30b, "He that winneth souls is wise" (KJV).

I am today what Mother made me. She has been my teacher, my counselor, my mentor, and the portrait of God in our home. My mother will be remembered by thousands of people as a soul winner, and she will be remembered by thousands of church members as a pastor's wife who was the reason for her husband's success.

Dad was a brilliant introvert who loved books and loved to preach, but people in general were not his forte. Every hospital call was made with my mother. She would do the talking, the comforting, the counseling, and then Dad would pray. In his presence, she would plan the church calendar and resolve church conflicts with a diplomatic flair.

Because of all these things, she will be remembered by her sons as an angel from Heaven whom God gave to us to shape our lives for His service. I am living today the lessons my mother taught me to be as a child.

As of this writing, Mother is ninety-one years old and has served the Lord with all of her heart, soul, mind, and body from her sixteenth year of life. The principles of her faith are the fortress in which she lives. As in the familiar phrase "The longer she serves the Lord, the sweeter He becomes to her," her prayer life is stronger than it has ever been, and I know that her prayers still make a difference in my life. When I am in spiritual warfare, Mother is the first person I phone. From her house, Heaven is a local call.

LESSON TWENTY

MAMAS TEACH US THAT IT'S NEVER TOO LATE

Actually, I learned this lesson from my grandmother, Father's mother, a great lady by the name of Lorena Gray, who lived in Hattiesburg, Mississippi. She was a stout woman, about five feet seven, with a very large breast and a large mole on the side of her face. She was a hard worker with rather masculine hands, whose life was spent doing whatever it took to make things happen. She outlived three husbands — one who was murdered and two who died of natural causes. She was also a very kind woman whose strength was mammoth and whose heart was good. She was a church woman, an African Methodist Episcopal church woman, to be exact.

I called her Grandma, but lest that term cause you to envision a sappy-sweet lady who sat back and greeted everything life brought her with a smile and a Scripture, let me share with you a description of what my grandma was really like and what made her so dear to me. The reason she stands out, the reason I so admire her, is that she absolutely refused to live her life without realizing her dream. She had the strength, the drive, the determination, the defiance, the perseverance, and the patience to climb over every mountainous obstacle before her and to reach the point where she could point to her life's target and say, "Bulls-eye."

You might say that my mother inherited her dream of having a college education and then being able to teach others from her mother, because Grandma had the dream long before she had my mother. Grandma could not pursue her dreams of higher learning at an age we would consider appropriate today, but she did not let the dream go as days and months and years passed. She never accepted the fact that she would not be able to go to college; she simply stayed focused on her life's goal until she reached it, even though it took her nearly fifty years.

To fund her education, she spent years washing white people's clothes and then sent them back sparkling. She had to do extra work — often, I'm sure, until her muscles ached, her fingers bled, and she was so tired she could hardly move. She had to scrimp and save and sacrifice — then scrimp and save and sacrifice some more. But then, at last, in her late forties, my grandmother knew it was time for her to contact the college and inquire about admission. What a day that must have been for her! She went through the required process and was informed that she could begin her coursework when the next semester commenced. She worked hard and studied diligently until the long-awaited day arrived. She graduated when she was half a century old! Armed with her degree, she then proceeded to land a teaching job and taught to her heart's content until she reached retirement age.

By the time my grandmother passed away, she had purchased her own home and had money in the bank — remarkable achievements for an African American woman in her day! But not only had she achieved those distinctions and personal rewards, she had also reached the admirable goal of having deposited knowledge and wisdom and skills in the minds of hundreds of people during her tenure in the classroom.

As Grandma fulfilled her dream as a teacher, she helped people fulfill their dreams too — dreams they could never have realized without the lessons they learned from her. Just think, if she had not pursued her dream with such tenacity, so many young people would have missed the lessons she taught in the unique way she presented them. Beyond that, though, they would have also missed their exposure to the inspiration that she was — and then maybe they would not have been so inspired to do some of the things they have done. For hundreds of students over the years, she was not only a teacher, she was a living, breathing message whose life continually proclaimed, "You *can* do it! Don't you *dare* give up on that dream! It is not too late! It is *never* too late!" I have no doubt that many of her students are living productive, fulfilled lives today because of what they learned from her. And I have no doubt that some of them have achieved what seemed impossible simply because they knew that she did.

In a society in which age is such a factor and we are so conscious of the time clock and the body clock, my grandmother reminds me — and I hope she reminds you too — that it is never too late to pursue a dream. She had to hold her dream in her heart for many years. She had to wait for it and she had to work for it, but she never gave up on it. I come from generations of people who never gave up on their dreams, but this story about my grandmother, her college degree, and her teaching career is one of the most inspiring true-life tales of them all.

I have written this remarkable tale about my grandmother not because I needed to share it, but because I believed it could accomplish something good in your life. I hope her story will light a fire in your heart and put a fresh wind beneath your wings. I pray that it will cause you to take some of your dreams out of the closet of your heart, blow the dust off them, and declare that they will live again. Nothing would make me happier than for you to get busy working toward those goals you had almost forgotten, or for you to begin taking steps, finally, toward the fulfillment of your dream.

Whether your dream is grand or simple, you may meet some opposition as you pursue it. People may tell you that it is too late, that you should not waste your time. Brush it off! Somewhere in the pit of their hearts, these folks probably wish they had your courage. If you can believe in God, believe in yourself, and believe in your dreams, you do not need anyone else's consent.

Do not ever give up on your dream. Whatever you really want to achieve, to possess, to conquer, to discover, or to enjoy — go for it, and inspire others along the way. Let them see your dedication, your persistence, and your victory when you reach your goal. Tell them that they can fulfill their dreams too. Do what you can to help them. Determine that no dream is going to die in the hearts of those you love, not on your watch. Encourage them to go for it as soon as they can, even if they are fifty, sixty, or seventy. If they are still breathing, inspire them to do something great!

Homework for the heart: How have your grandparents inspired you to realize that it's never too late? What did they accomplish late in life that continues to encourage you in your journey? Is there something that you have dismissed because you're "too old" or it's "too late"? What do you need to do to get started on it today?

A mother's secret prayer: Dear Lord, I pray that I would never give in to a spirit of defeat and despair. I ask that You would always help me take the next step and then the next one, knowing with You that all things are possible. May I realize that it's never too late to fulfill the calling You have placed within me and to move closer to the dreams which You have planted in my heart. I pray that my example will inspire my children to know that Your timing goes beyond our mistakes and delays. Amen.

LESSON TWENTY-ONE
MAMAS TEACH US TO LIVE OUT OUR LEGACY

Toward the end of her life, my mother looked up at me one day and said, "The only thing that got old on me was my body." I smiled and knew what she meant, already experiencing for myself the creaking joints and blurring eyesight that had signaled my descent into middle age. Her comment also reminded me that even as our bodies sag and age before our eyes each morning in our bathroom mirrors, there is something timeless inside of us. God has created us as spiritual beings with immortal souls. But our awareness of this quality, this sense of having eternity in our hearts, as the Preacher in Ecclesiastes calls it, echoes far beyond the moment in time where we find ourselves today. And our mothers lived out of this awareness, turning each day's simple song into an echo across the chasm of eternity.

This entire book has been written as a tribute to our mothers and the invaluable lessons that they have taught us. Whether they come from my mother, your mother, other mothers, or biblical mothers, these lessons provide an amazing cumulative legacy of guiding principles that continue to serve us well through this wonder-and-worry-filled journey of life. But the fact of the matter is that I wouldn't be writing this book and you wouldn't be reading it if our mothers had not lived out their legacy in front of us over the course of their lifetime and ours. If their actions undermined their instruction, then we would discard it like spoiled milk.

If our mothers only told us these lessons on life, love, and longevity, and did not live them out in the flesh-and-blood trials and tribulations of everyday life, complete with unexpected illness, overdue mortgage payments, societal indifference, and personal disappointment, then we wouldn't want to pass them on. No, to forge a legacy, you must live out of it long during your lifetime, long before the words and acts become the building stones for a dwelling place to shelter future generations. Our mothers owned the responsibility of not only living for their present families but for their grandchildren and great-grandchildren yet to come. They instinctively know and live out of the soul wisdom that what they do each day becomes larger than the sum of its parts.

Scripture is certainly consistent about reminding us that we will reap what we sow, and for many of us, our mothers sowed beautiful seeds of truth, wisdom, joy, and peace, a spiritual harvest that is now bearing fruit in us and in our children. As we come to the close of this book and prepare to peek inside the Motherhood Hall of Fame, my prayer for you is that you have learned something you didn't know before, that you have gained an appreciation of all that your mother sacrificed for your benefit, and that you will now pass along these lessons to your own children and those around you. Mothers have always made a difference and will continue to do so for as long as their babies are being born on this planet. My hope is that we will be worthy of their investment and return a dividend that honors them and their memory as well as glorifies God.

If your mother is still living, I encourage you to call her and tell her what a difference she has made in your life. If she has already passed away, then I encourage you to write her a letter, expressing all the things that the two of you did not get a chance to discuss. Build from her legacy and launch yourself into your life with exuberant passion to accomplish the mighty things that she saw in you, back when she held you in her arms. Make her proud by fulfilling the dreams that she started but did not bring to completion. And along the way, plant the seeds of dreams in your own children, knowing that someday, when you are beyond this earth, they will be carrying your legacy with them, completing what you started.

Homework for the heart: How would you describe your mother's legacy to you? What do you want your legacy to be for your children or those you love? What do you need to change in your life to fulfill your potential? How can you begin this process today?

A mother's secret prayer: Dear God, I ask that my legacy might be based on how I live my life, not just what I tell my children to do. Please use my dreams to further the dreams of my children so that they might build a bridge to their own children, passing the generational torch of godliness and greatness from one to another. Amen

CONCLUSION

A PEEK INTO THE MOTHERHOOD
HALL OF FAME

Throughout human history, in every culture, men and women, boys and girls have had a special place in their hearts for their mothers. Children run to them when they are sad or afraid; adults turn to them for counsel and guidance, a listening ear, or encouragement when the going gets tough.

In this final chapter, I would like to share with you a sampling of what others have said about their mothers. I offer you poignant paragraphs and brief stories as a potpourri of praise to the great women known and loved as mothers over more than two hundred years of American history, up until the present, and from cultures around the world.

A Jewish proverb rightly affirms what most of us have experienced: "A mother understands what a child does not say." I cannot fully explain the dynamics that exist between a mother and her children, but I do know

397

that mothers can hear sentences in the silences of their children; they can see disappointment or sadness in their children's posture or gestures; they can perceive mischief or guilt in the tone of a voice or in the certain way little feet shuffle through a room. No, children do not need words to be able to communicate effectively to their mothers because these intuitive women do indeed understand what children do not say.

An old Spanish saying makes me chuckle, but I know it is true: "An ounce of mother is worth a pound of priests." If you have ever heard a mother pray for her children or had a mother pray for you, you also know that this is true. Nobody prays like a mama prays. A mother's prayers are a priceless gift, a real treasure, an earnest, heartfelt force of unspeakable power and of worth that is only known in heaven. If you have a mother who prays for you, you are blessed indeed.

James Russell Lowell, the American poet and man of letters who was so highly regarded for his intellect that he secured a position as professor at Harvard University during the 1800s, declared that the best teachers of all are our mothers when he wrote: "That best academy, a mother's knee."

Booker T. Washington was born into

slavery in 1856, but he later became a highly influential educator and leader, an adviser to two U.S. presidents, and the founder of Tuskegee Institute. He certainly had a remarkable life, full of great achievements, and in reflecting upon his life, he said: "If I have done anything in life worth attention, I feel sure that I inherited the disposition from my mother." I believe that sentiment is true for many of us. The ability to accomplish worthy goals — and the encouragement we need along the way — does so often come from our mothers.

Let me also call your attention to the words of Washington Irving, an American diplomat and writer perhaps best known for his *Legend of Sleepy Hollow* and story of Rip Van Winkle. He wrote: "A mother is the truest friend we have, when trials, heavy and sudden, fall upon us; when adversity takes the place of prosperity; when friends who rejoice with us in our sunshine, desert us when troubles thicken around us, still will she cling to us, and endeavor by her kind precepts and counsels to dissipate the clouds of darkness, and cause peace to return to our hearts." He is right, and I am sure you can think of many times when your mother has proven more faithful and more valuable to you than any other colleague or comrade. It's the truth, our mothers really are, in many ways, our truest friends.

Now, for the remainder of this chapter, I want to shine the spotlight on the mothers of some great Americans, most of whom I trust you will be acquainted with through their accomplishments in the areas of music and entertainment, athletics, social change, and ministry.

B. B. KING

Recently, during one of my partner's conferences, I met one of the children of the amazing and legendary musician B. B. King. This daughter spoke of her dad with love and affection. Her passion for him is a great reflection of how we should always love those who poured so much into us. In that same spirit of gratitude, I wanted you to hear what he says about his own parent, his mother, and her role in strengthening him.

In *Blues All Around Me: The Autobiography of B. B. King,* he writes:

There's a moment in our life together I've never forgotten, a time when she prepared me for a visit to a grieving family. Their mother had died and the body, on display in their cabin, was to be embalmed the next day. The body had been dressed for viewing. "But don't stare," Mama said, "and don't eat up all the food.". . .

It's creepy in the cabin. The dead body is scary, and I don't know where to look or what to say. My uneasiness makes me hungry. I eat a few cookies but when I see the potato pies on the other side of the table, I go right to them. I'm just about to put that pie in my mouth — it's pipin' hot and smells delicious — when Mama gives me a look. I think it means *Stop eating,* but I want the pie. It's about the size of a saucer, and I slip it in my pocket. I sit down and, man, that sucker starts burning my leg. I can't do nothing but cry. . . .

"What's wrong with you, boy?" Mama wants to know.

I can't say; I just stammer and look down. Mama won't have it. She takes me outside and demands an explanation. I look up and say, "I'm sorry, Mama, I know you d-d-d-d-d-didn't want me to eat no m-m-m-m-more, so I snuck this pie." . . . She has me slip off my shorts and sees how the heat's burned off my skin. . . . "Oh, baby," she says, "you took my look the wrong way. I didn't mean for you not to eat. You don't need to be scared of your mama." And with that, she apologized. But more than apologized, she started crying along with me. She was as hurt as me. We were deeply connected; our hearts were joined together.[1]

HELEN KELLER

In her autobiography, *The Story of My Life,* Helen Keller writes of the early days after her illness left her deaf and blind:

I cannot recall what happened during the first months after my illness. I only know that I sat in my mother's lap or hung to her dress as she went about her household duties. My hands felt every object and observed every motion, and in this way I learned to know many things. Soon I felt the need of some communication with others and began to make crude signs. A shake of the head meant "No" and a nod, "Yes," a pull meant "Come" and a push "Go." Was it bread that I wanted? Then I would imitate the acts of cutting the slices and buttering them. If I wanted my mother to make ice-cream for dinner I made the sign for working the freezer and shivered, indicating cold. My mother, moreover, succeeded in making me understand a good deal. I always knew when she wished me to bring her something, and I would run upstairs or anywhere else she indicated. Indeed, I owe to her loving wisdom all that was bright and good in my long night.[2]

DOROTHY HEIGHT

Dr. Dorothy Height, more than ninety years old at the writing of this book, is one of the great heroes of the civil rights movement and of the advancement of black women in the United States. A friend and source of counsel to U.S. presidents from Eisenhower to Clinton, this champion of freedom and justice has been awarded the Presidential Medal of Freedom, the Congressional Gold Medal, the Franklin Delano Roosevelt Freedom Medal, and the Citizens Medal Award. Besides that, Dorothy Height is the recipient of our own Woman of Purpose award, which was presented to her at the MegaFest event in 2004. She is a personal friend of mine and a lady of considerable distinction. Her classy demeanor and bright intellect serve as a perpetual beacon to this nation of what can be done when education and effort fuse together with tenacity and perseverance.

She tells the following story about her

mother, Fannie Burroughs Height, in her memoir, *Open Wide the Freedom Gates:*

My mother helped me understand how not to show off what I knew, but how to use it so that others might benefit. She always kept before me my responsibility to other people, and she taught me the importance of being cooperative instead of competitive. But she did make me compete with myself and always perform upward. When I brought home my report card, she would ask, "What happened? Last time you made 92. This time you made 90." I'd protest that 90 was the best grade in the class. "I did not ask what other people did," my mother would reply. "I want to know about Dorothy Height. What happened that she didn't do as well as she did last time?" Even today, after I make some kind of public presentation, I have to evaluate it for myself. I want to give everything my best because when you do that, you get much more than you give. That's one of my mother's lasting legacies.[3]

SIDNEY POITIER

The legendary actor, writer, and director

writes in his biography, *The Measure of a Man,* a brief, poignant story about growing up on a place in the Bahamas, called Cat Island, and learning to swim.

Cat Island is forty-six miles long and three miles wide, and even as a small child I was free to roam anywhere. I climbed trees by myself at four and five years old and six and seven years old. I would get attacked by wasps, and I would go home with both eyes closed from having been stung on the face over and over. I would be crying and hollering and screaming and petrified, and my mom would take me and treat me with bush medicines from the old culture that you wouldn't believe, and then I would venture back out and go down to the water and fish alone.

I would even go in sometimes and swim by myself. I had the confidence, because when I was very small my mother threw me in the ocean and watched without moving as I struggled to survive. She watched as I screamed, yelled, gulped, and flailed in a panic-stricken effort to stay afloat. She watched as I clawed desperately at the water, unable to manage more than a few seconds before starting to sink beneath the surface. She watched as the ocean swallowed me, second by second. Then, mercifully, my father's hands reached under, fished me out, and handed me back up to my mother . . . who threw me back in again, and again and again, until she was convinced that I knew how to swim.[4]

DENZEL WASHINGTON

Recently, I was privileged to meet Denzel Washington and his praying mother. It was such a blessing to be invited to the premiere of the Broadway production of *Julius Caesar*. In it, Denzel did an incredible job in his starring role as Marcus Brutus. After the stunning performance, I was whisked to a reception, where his lovely mother and I shared a pleasant conversation. Later, when I spoke with the actor himself, I could see the many similarities of faith and fire that passed down to him through his parents.

In an interview with CBS in April 2005, he described growing up in his family and his mother's emphasis on education. When he was fourteen years old, his mother had saved enough money to send him to Oakland Academy, a small boarding school for boys in New York.

"I was in public school, Mount Vernon

High School, and my mother decided it was best to get me out of there before I ended up where a lot of my friends are now — you know, in the grave, in the penitentiary."

After his mother visited him at school and informed him that she and his father were getting a divorce, he recalls becoming angry. "I think I started getting in a little trouble after that. Started getting in fights." These fights led to disciplinary measures that almost had him removed from the school, but his mother stepped in and her talk with the headmaster led them to change their minds.

"I owe her everything," says Washington.[5]

JAMAL BRYANT

One of the fastest-growing churches in America is Empowerment Temple in Baltimore. The senior pastor and visionary leader of this dynamic congregation is my friend Dr. Jamal-Harrison Bryant. Some call him radical; he is called to a new generation and is not afraid to implement new ideas. Others call him revolutionary because of his ability to think outside of the box. Personally, I see him as a gifted young man whose potential influence is limited only by his focus and consecration to the task set before him. I call him an effective agent for social change, a catalyst for economic empowerment, and a champion who fights tirelessly to see individuals reach their full potential in every area of their lives.

While traveling with me to Africa, where I was going to do some philanthropic work in Kenya, he clearly explained his influences that were passed on through a rich and extensive legacy of faith. I wanted you to have the rich experience of sitting back with a cup of coffee and hearing the conversation as this extraordinary young man talks about his Mama.

Noted educator, writer, and lecturer Dr. Jawanza Kunjufu wrote a riveting work entitled *To Be Popular or Smart: The Black Peer Group* (African American Images, 1988). In it, he discussed how African American males often excel and do well until the sixth grade, when they have to make the unfortunate decision to be popular or to be smart. Regrettably, I chose the former. Conveniently, it seemed as if I somehow ended up in a fight, on suspension, or in the principal's office whenever my dad was out of town. On one such occasion, my mother picked me up from school and, just when I thought she was going to backhand me, blurted out to the Lord with tears in her eyes, "God, I'm giving him back to you. I can't do anything else with him. Don't kill him, but bring him close enough to death for him to reevaluate life!"

Talk about a Damascus road experience! Hearing my mother offer me as a sacrifice with no ram in the bush in sight was startling, to say the least. Needless to say, I was never suspended, nor did I ever have another fight after that day because I wanted to live! I could also see that I was killing my mother on the inside. Years later, I founded the "Stop the Violence, Start the Love" campaign through the NAACP after the killings of rappers Notorious BIG and Tupac Shakur, because I knew what their mothers and thousands of others were feeling.

When I was in the eleventh grade in the city-wide gifted and talented program, my grades slipped because jokes were my major, while girls became my minor. My GPA had so plummeted that the school authorities were kicking me out of the school or forcing me to repeat the grade. In our exit interview, the teacher told my parents, "Jamal has a problem. He can't decide whether he wants to be Eddie Murphy or Martin Luther King, Jr. Don't waste your money on college. Just put him in trade school."

My mother, a sanctified revolutionary with an Afro, declared, "The devil is a liar! You must not know the God who can turn this around." I subsequently received my GED, my bachelor's degree from Morehouse College, my master's from Duke University, and my doctorate of ministry from Oxford University in Great Britain.

During my second year of seminary, President Kweisi Mfume tapped me to be the National Youth and College Director of the NAACP. I was to lead sixty thousand young people from around the world to pick up the banner for civil rights. I was the youngest person ever to hold that position, and the rules had been bent so that I could run the organization while still being a full-time student. I was only twenty-three years old!

During Christmas break that year, I discovered that my girlfriend was pregnant. There I was, a seminarian and a role model to sixty thousand young people. Depression was ever-present, moral failure was obvious, and embarrassment was an understatement. All the more, I'm a third-generation preacher. *Do I quit the ministry?* I wondered. *Do I leave the NAACP?* I was unsure.

I woke up in the middle of the night and found my mother praying at the edge of the bed. She told me the Lord showed her I was under attack, and whatever it was that I was dealing with, the family would see it through. I broke down in tears and told her of my moral failure. She said, "You stand in the company of David; therefore you can still be king."

I'm still reaching for the crown with a beautiful wife, two beautiful daughters, a seven-thousand-member church, and a God who looks beyond my faults and sees my needs — not to mention a mother who believed in redemption!

ROSA PARKS

I want to take a moment before we close this chapter to focus on and celebrate a woman who never bore or raised children of her own, but whose actions, influence, and position in society birthed entire generations into freedom and justice. Let me first acknowledge that many women enter into motherhood intentionally. They dream of having children, they plan, they pay attention to their biological clocks, they use

411

birth control when they are not ready to have children and discontinue its use when they are. Other women, of course, are surprised to find out that "something is in the oven." All expectant women, though, have roughly nine months to prepare to become mothers. Not so Rosa Parks. She never intended to become the mother of a movement that would change the entire fabric of a society for the better, but she did. She is indeed the mother of the civil rights movement. She did not seek such a maternal position, but her action on the bus assured it.

The person most like a daughter to Rosa Parks is Elaine Steele, who, as a high school student, met Mrs. Parks while both of them were working in a sewing factory during the 1960s and whose assistance I greatly appreciate in this portion of the book. Through the years, Elaine Steele attended to Mrs. Parks in a variety of ways, including serving as her manager in the midst of a busy schedule of speaking and public appearances, and cofounded the Rosa and Raymond Parks Institute for Self-Development with Mrs. Parks in 1987. Though Rosa Parks is not here with us anymore, I want to pay tribute to a woman for whom I have limitless respect and to Ms. Steele, for her role in caring for Mrs. Parks.

I remember how honored I was when I met Mrs. Parks for the first time, several years ago. By then, her body was confined to a wheelchair, but I could sense the strength in her soul. She was soft-spoken, gentle, and dainty, but I knew that she had moved a mountain — the mountain of racial inequality and injustice — in her earlier days. Surely, the civil rights movement had many heroes and leaders, but she had started it all.

Some say she was tired from working at her job as a seamstress that first day of December 1955, when she refused to obey a law that required her to rise from her seat on a Montgomery, Alabama, bus. She was sitting in the back of the bus, in what they called the "colored" section, which was reserved for black people — unless a white person wanted a seat. When she did not move from her seat to allow a white man to sit down, she broke the law — but she knew that particular law needed to be broken. Describing the incident in her own words, she writes quite simply in her little children's book, *I Am Rosa Parks:* "I was tired of black people being pushed around. Some people think I kept my seat because I'd had a hard day, but that is not true. I was just tired of giving in."[6]

By staying seated, the saying goes, Mrs. Parks stood up for an entire race of people who were being treated in ways that were grossly unfair. Her action that day got her arrested, but it eventually led to the end of legalized segregation in America. All of us who affirm the dignity of every living being and who believe in "justice for all" owe a great debt to Mrs. Rosa Parks, the mother of the civil rights movement in the United States and a heroine of liberty and equality in the hearts of people everywhere who love freedom and fairness.

When Mrs. Parks passed away in October 2005, the entire world took notice. In the United States, she became the first woman to lie in honor in the United States Capitol building, making history once again, even in death. I especially appreciate the words of the media release distributed upon her death, which so beautifully and aptly describe the character and life of this great lady: "Mrs. Parks was a woman who exhibited dignity with pride, courage with perseverance, and an ever-present quiet strength."[7]

I hope you have enjoyed this journey through modern history and these snapshots of women who have truly made a difference as they have mothered. Let me encourage you today, especially if you are knee-deep in diapers and covered in baby food, you may be raising the next great world leader, entertainer, scientist, or athletic superstar. Greatness may be living under your roof and crawling on your floors — just waiting for you to nurture and develop it. Never underestimate your influence, my sister, for mothers really do make a difference.

NOTES

1. B. B. King and David Ritz, *Blues All Around Me: The Autobiography of B. B. King* (New York: Avon, 1996), 18–19.
2. Helen Keller, *The Story of My Life* (New York: Bantam, 1990), 5–6.
3. Dorothy Height, *Open Wide the Freedom Gates* (New York: Public Affairs, 2003), 14–15.
4. Sidney Poitier, *The Measure of a Man* (New York: Harper Collins, 2000), 3, 4.
5. "From Hollywood to Broadway: Ed Bradley Talks to Actor Denzel Washington," CBSNews, April 20, 2005, www.cbsnews.com, accessed September 29, 2005.
6. Rosa Parks, *I Am Rosa Parks* (New York: Puffin Books, 1997), 28.
7. www.rosaparks.org.

ABOUT THE AUTHOR

Bishop T. D. Jakes is founder and senior pastor of the 28,000-member Potter's House congregation in Dallas. He is the bestselling author of numerous books, including *He-Motions; The 10 Commandments of Working in a Hostile Environment; The Lady, Her Lover and Her Lord; Maximize the Moment; The Great Investment; God's Leading Lady; Woman, Thou Art Loosed!* and *His Lady.* He has been honored by *Time* magazine as "America's Best Preacher" and has been featured in *The Wall Street Journal* and *People.* Bishop Jakes has appeared on *Larry King Live;* earned Grammy nominations for his music CDs; and produced a full-length film, *Woman, Thou Art Loosed!* which was a prizewinner at the Santa Barbara Film Festival. His anointed message of healing and restoration, in demand by clergy and laity alike, transcends every cultural and denominational barrier. Bishop Jakes's weekly television outreach, *The Potter's House*, has become a favorite throughout America, Africa, Australia, the Caribbean, and Europe. His daily television program, *The Potter's Touch,* can be viewed on TBN and BET.

The employees of Thorndike Press hope you have enjoyed this Large Print book. All our Thorndike and Wheeler Large Print titles are designed for easy reading, and all our books are made to last. Other Thorndike Press Large Print books are available at your library, through selected bookstores, or directly from us.

For information about titles, please call:
(800) 223-1244

or visit our Web site at:

www.gale.com/thorndike
www.gale.com/wheeler

To share your comments, please write:

Publisher
Thorndike Press
295 Kennedy Memorial Drive
Waterville, ME 04901